Pagan Portals

Ishtar and Ereshkigal

The Daughters of Sin

Scott Irvine

MOON
BOOKS

Winchester, UK
Washington, USA

JOHN HUNT PUBLISHING

First published by Moon Books, 2020
Moon Books is an imprint of John Hunt Publishing Ltd., No. 3 East Street, Alresford
Hampshire SO24 9EE, UK
office@jhpbooks.net
www.johnhuntpublishing.com
www.moon-books.net

For distributor details and how to order please visit the 'Ordering' section on our website.

Text copyright: Scott Irvine 2019

ISBN: 978 1 78904 321 1
978 1 78904 322 8 (ebook)
Library of Congress Control Number: 2019938348

A CIP catalogue record for this book is available from the British Library.

Design: Stuart Davies

UK: Printed and bound by CPI Group (UK) Ltd, Croydon, CR0 4YY
US: Printed and bound by Thomson-Shore, 7300 West Joy Road, Dexter, MI 48130

We operate a distinctive and ethical publishing philosophy in all areas of our business, from our global network of authors to production and worldwide distribution.

Pagan Portals

Ishtar and Ereshkigal

The Daughters of Sin

Contents

dedicated to my late mum
Shirley Ann Howell
who made this book possible

Foreword

I am sitting on the innermost and highest rampart of Maiden Castle, a Bronze Age Hillfort on the outskirts of Dorchester in the heart of the Dorset countryside. The fort was constructed and occupied by the Celts from around 600BCE up until it was overcome by the Roman general Vespasian forty-three years after the birth of Christ. The morning is overcast and a cold breeze is sweeping across the landscape making itself known to my exposed face and hands. Dark rainclouds are pressing in from the southwest. The old Roman road, now the busy A354 between Dorchester and Weymouth, is hidden behind the tree line in the distance and far enough away from noise and pollution. Surrounding fields dissected by a patchwork of ancient Saxon hedgerows meet the grey sky in all directions looking much as it did thirteen hundred years ago. South of here just over the brow of a hill is the ancient Ridgeway, now the South West Coastal Path connecting Abbotsbury in the west to Osmington in the east, skirting above the low lying district of Weymouth and stretching down towards the rocky outcrop of Portland and the English Channel. A buzzard glides effortlessly on the breeze overhead in search of breakfast.

I am in nature surrounded by the elements and slowly drifting back through time, through space and through history, back to when the Celts lived, worked and played here. Every now and again, when I can, I like to escape the hustle and bustle of the busy modern world to wind down the stress levels and emotions and just sit and be. Any time of year is a good time to be out in the fresh air sharing time with nature and experience the interaction of the elements through the five senses. I feel the cold air caress my bare skin and with each breath, I can taste the salty sea air. I can smell the distinct aroma of the nearby farms and hear above the sound of the wind the occasional loud exhaust of a motorbike making its way through the traffic and the distinctive caw of a crow drifting in and out of earshot as it flies over the fort.

As I immerse myself in the landscape, the heavy cloud breaks allowing a moment of sunshine to cast out the gloomy light over Maiden Castle and replace it with light and shadow. Then it is gone again, hidden once more behind the sea of grey.

The interplay of light and dark remind me of two of the earliest goddesses we know of from Sumerian and Babylonian clay tablets written over 5,000 years ago; the goddess of life, Ishtar and her sister Ereshkigal, the goddess of death. I discovered the sisters through the Celtic Brigit and Cailleach, their ancient whispers reaching out through time in the shadows of the light and darkness of the day. Ishtar and Ereshkigal have become overshadowed by the classical goddesses we are familiar with today, their memories hidden in the thick mists of time waiting to be heard once more.

The Mesopotamian flesh and blood gods and goddesses were called the Anunnaki, which means 'those from heaven to earth came', and they were the first deities we know of to have human form and personalities, attitudes and emotions that we can relate to today. The sisters Ishtar and Ereshkigal have a very interesting story to tell. It journeys through space and time, through history and through cultures. The daughters of Sin, the Babylonian God of the Moon, reveal themselves in both the physical and spiritual realms as we search for their light and dark powers hidden in plain sight once you know where to look. They can be found well away from the modern world of busy-ness and pollution at ancient sites, in the countryside and in forests and besides rivers and lakes and in parks and gardens. The sisters can be found anywhere in nature where we can discover the balance that will bring harmony into our lives.

Ishtar, as Inanna was the original goddess of love and forerunner to all the fertility goddesses that follow. Know Ishtar and you will understand Aphrodite and Venus better. Know Ereshkigal and you will understand Persephone and Cailleach better. Together Ishtar and Ereshkigal are the opposing nature of the feminine force both physically and spiritually and are the change that allows growth and evolution to occur on Earth, the interaction between life, death and rebirth.

There is plenty of information on Ishtar and Ereshkigal in books where different people give different accounts of the stories depending on how the clay tablets were interpreted. The stories relate to events that have been passed down by word of mouth for thousands of years before the invention of writing. Some have been spiced up for dramatic interest but remember it is always the victor that records history to suit the power and glory of their god and king. The stories were told to appeal to the population; even back then the people would have enjoyed the entertainment. Like us today they would have liked to be enthralled and at times scared and on the edge of their cushion or mat in suspense. For the priests it was a way to encourage the community into the temple to honour the city deity and bring offerings for the priests to pass on to the gods and goddesses who were busy protecting the state from danger.

While tribes in Europe were building great stone temples like Carnac in Brittany and Avebury on the chalk downs of Wiltshire, Mesopotamia was constructing giant brick ziggurat temples, palaces and cities where stone was scarce and irrigating parched land so that grain and cattle could thrive in the desert. On top of that, technology 5,000 years ago allowed their gods and goddesses to fly across the sky in fiery chariots, and had they staffs that could shoot lightning at an enemy and magic that could bring the dead back to life. However, like all things that exist in the material world even the gods and goddesses grow old and weak. When a new wave of empires rose in Europe around 800BC the Anunnaki deities reinvented themselves to become the likes of Zeus, Venus, Shiva, Odin, Lugh, Thor, Brigit,

Apollo, Diane and Shakti to name a few.

The cold chill is starting to penetrate my jacket and I am aware of other visitors admiring the views from Maiden Castle. It is time to get back home and finish my writing. Cutting through the camp, I pass the foundations of a Romano-Celtic temple built 300 years after the Roman invasion. In all probabilities, the temple would have been dedicated to Venus or some aspect of her. Coming out of the path through the ramparts down to the car park where my motorbike waits I feel blessed. My spirit has been energised by the visit and my heart is happy. I have touched the soul of the ancient site and am now ready to return to the 21st Century.

Hail and Welcome
Samhain 2018

Mystery of the Planets

The Neolithic priest kings of Sumer, the first civilization to become a powerful empire after the biblical flood, were very aware of the influence on the human mind of the celestial bodies that floated across the heavens. This knowledge gave them great power within society. They understood the impact that each heavenly body had on everything that lived on the planet and through observation, used that knowledge to have great influence over the population.

With the arrival of the metal ages came writing on clay tablets by priestly scribes that reveal the daily lives of the Sumerian people 5,000 years ago. They not only recorded their laws, business records and promises but also told epic tales of gods and goddesses whose will the populations obeyed without question. Earth's 'orbiting' celestial bodies that included the Sun and the Moon were humankind's earliest deities with human personalities and emotions, an invisible influence with a physical manifestation on Earth. These planet powers had to be honoured and worshipped by humankind who were busy working for their community while the priest kings grew in importance, power and wealth.

According to the cuneiform tablets the early gods and goddesses were called Anunnaki, 'those from heaven to earth came' whose arrival led to humanity learning language, the ability to control fire and create intricate stone tools to skin and butcher prey for food, clothing and shelter. Their endeavours were watched and guided by the major Anunnaki gods and goddesses governing the solar system from heaven within the circling planets. Each planet was a god or goddess depending on which way they span on their axis giving the earth six brothers and one sister, each with an individual influence over the human race, each a different personality felt within the human mind as they race around the Sun. So, who were the Anunnaki planetary gods and goddess?

Let us begin with the sole woman in the family, Ishtar. As a single woman in a brood of brothers, the goddess had to be strong, cunning and know how to use her femininity and beauty so she could be heard among her brothers. Ishtar was sister to both the Sun God Shamash and the Queen of Death, Ereshkigal whose father was the Moon God, Sin. As the only feminine celestial influence, there was no contest for the role of the divine being of Love and fertility. She was a beautiful goddess and feisty with it. With her raging tempers, Ishtar often challenged the aggression of her sister's husband Nergal, the God of War. To the conquering Babylonians Ishtar was the Morning Star, the Light Bearer, aka Lucifer, ushering in the Mesopotamian New Year (Akitu) and the fertility that the flooding of the Euphrates brought to the land.

When the power of Greece became the world leader in influence almost three thousand years ago, Ishtar transformed into the beautiful Aphrodite before becoming the Roman Venus five hundred years later.

The physical planet Venus is a cloud shrouded greenhouse world and Earth's nearest neighbour. She is about the same size as our world but hotter and toxic to humans. Her surface temperature is $480°$ C and has a carbon dioxide rich atmosphere ninety times denser than Earth's. A human standing on Venus would be instantly incinerated by the heat, crushed by the atmosphere and dissolved in sulphuric acid rain. Do not judge a planet by its outer appearance; it is what is within the outer shell that counts and the essence at the heart of all planets as it is with ourselves. Venus spins very slowly on her axis and in the opposite direction to her brothers and comes within 24 million miles of Earth during her orbit of 225 days at a distance of 67 Million miles from the Sun.

The influence of Venus governs the human body as a whole

but in particular the lower back. She underscores the feminine aspect of the human personality and encourages the spiritual side of love. Venus can bestow gentleness, friendship and diplomacy but beware of her dark side and her issues with anger and revenge.

Ishtar's brother was the impartial God of the Sun, Shamash, who sat in judgment over the actions of both gods and humanity. He became the Greek Helios who was associated with music and prophecy, becoming Sol, or Sun of the Roman world from which all the other planets received their energy. It is the Sun that pushes back the darkness from the solar system and warms Mother Earth (whom incidentally spins in the same direction as the masculine planets so therefore must have a male influence on the human consciousness). The sun brings fertility and life to the sacred planet and energy to the rest of the solar system.

Our Sun sits 93 million miles away from earth with his light taking about nine minutes to reach us. It is a gas giant of hydrogen and helium with a fluid electromagnetic core burning at 15,000,000°C cooling to around 6,000°C at the surface releasing a particle wind through the entire solar system producing huge solar flares that can affect the weather and electronics on Earth.

The Moon God, Sin, was the father of the celestial Ishtar and Shamash and the Underworld queen Ereshkigal. Sin ruled over time until Kronos stole it away, and was the seasonal calendar the priests worked to. Sin was the protector of cattle, ensuring the fertility of the farmsteads for food and trade. The other Gods consulted him for his wisdom and, to many, Sin was the supreme god of the heavens with his influence on Earth being the strongest of all the 'planets'. For the Greeks, Earth's tiny satellite was the very feminine Artemis, the Goddess of the Hunt. Not only a name change but a sex change too. Was it because of her association with the 28 day menstruation cycle of women or the fact that the Greeks realised that although appearing to show only one face towards earth, the Moon was spinning on her axis in the same direction as the Goddess of Love, so must be female? The Romans called her Diane, a virgin goddess and protector of forests and women in childbirth.

The Moon is tiny compared to the Earth and orbits every 28 days or so getting to within 221,000 miles of us. The Moon represents the human subconscious and rules the chest and digestive system. She affects the emotions and ignites the imagination bringing patience and sympathy to humankind but can also be the cause of unreliable actions from unclear intentions.

The Sumerian war God was Ninurta whose symbol was the eagle and associated with thunderstorms, heavy rain and the spring floodwaters that gave life to the arid desert conditions of Mesopotamia. He held the 'Tablets of Law' and oversaw the fate and destiny of humanity. Ninurta fought alongside his warrior brother, Nergal, against the demons of chaos that threatened their world. For the Greeks he was the father of all gods, Kronos, who liked to eat his offspring before being banished to the underworld by his youngest son Zeus. Kronos was renamed Saturn by the Romans who is said to have taught humanity how to live a civilised way of life. His festival, the Saturnalia, was celebrated in Rome over the last seven days of December to celebrate the coming of a reborn Sun after the winter solstice. Saturn patrols the outer limit of the known solar system, a protective shield guarding the rest of the planets from the outside dangers of the universe. Saturn gives the potential for things to exist by transforming the formless into form. He is the God of Destruction whose influence contains the seeds of death.

The planet connects to the human skeleton particularly around the knees and feet. Although Saturn brings limitations and boundaries to the human mind, he also encourages honesty, common sense and loyalty.

Nergal, the God of Death ruled the underworld alongside

his wife Ereshkigal. He was the judge of the dead and God of Plagues, lord of both the fires of hell and the heat of the drought. The ancient texts reveal that when an ambassador of Ereshkigal arrived in her place to a feast for the elite, all the gods rose except Nergal. This angered the Underworld Queen who asked for his life. He appealed, of course, but was sentenced to make the journey to Ereshkigal to face execution by the evil eye. He took 14 warriors with him, one to guard each of the doors to her palace where he found the ambassador and killed him. Then he found Ereshkigal, dragged her to the floor and was about to slice off her head when she offered marriage and control of the underworld kingdom of the dead. Nergal relented, dried her tears and accepted her offer.

Nergal became the Greek God of War, Ares, and in turn the Roman Mars, whose month is March, the month associated with the rebirth of nature and the season for war. Mars gave the human mind assertiveness and passion.

Mars bestows the vital energy and sex drive that allows humanity to exist. He governs the head and encourages hard work, enthusiasm and courage but also shows a quick temper if he is felt hard done by.

The king of kings, Marduk, created order from chaos to make the world. He was the King of Heaven and the God of Justice on Earth. His father was the Lord of the Earth, Enki, and he took over Enki's duties, lording it over the earth when his father returned to the infinite source of the universe. The God of Justice transformed into the Greek Zeus, the Lord of all Heaven and father to humanity until the Romans renamed him Jupiter. The planet provides Rule and Justice to the earth and influences the human mind where knowledge, wisdom and philosophy are concerned and governs the thighs and liver. Jupiter encourages loyalty, justice and faithfulness. The King of the Gods is usually portrayed as an angry punishing god hurling thunderbolts towards anyone foolish enough to go against his wishes.

Marduk's son, Nabu, was a Babylonian priest king and the mediator between his father and humanity. He is associated with the Egyptian jackal headed god, Thoth, and succeeded by the Greek messenger god, Hermes, who helped to deliver the dead souls to the underworld. The Romans called him Mercury, the god of trade and commerce. He was associated with speed and communication and also deception.

The influence of Mercury is inspiration and social interaction and is the nearest planet to the sun and the smallest by some distance at only 3,000 miles in diameter. Mercury rules the hands, arms, lungs and the nervous system. He influences the intellect, communication and both physical and emotional energy. Mercury encourages quick thinking and good imagination but can also promote deceitfulness.

The planets dance and sing as they spiral through space and time, generating energy causing electromagnetic fields feeding the solar system as it journeys around the outer reaches of our galaxy. Our star, the individual planets, and their moons make up our solar system, one of many other solar systems that make up our galaxy, one of many galaxies that make up the universe, one of many universes that etc. etc.

The Cradle of Civilization

Before we get into the lives and personalities of Ishtar and Ereshkigal we need to understand the environment they existed in and the world that they were part of. The sisters were two of the major deities of the first civilisation to emerge from the Stone Age era in the Middle East around 3,500BCE called Sumer. The Neolithic people had migrated south from the cold mountainous regions following the Euphrates and Tigris rivers to settle in the fertile marshlands close to the Persian Gulf where both rivers met the sea. Their religion was based on the veneration of a holy trinity that consisted of the Father Moon God, the Son Sun God and the Holy Spirit of Venus, the goddess of the spring floods.

The fertile banks of the two rivers flooded the lowlands each spring coinciding with the return of Venus after a fifty-day absence. Farmers irrigated the low-lying land bringing water to the scorched summer ground to grow barley, wheat, dates and vegetables. The earth in which the crops grew was called Ninhursaga, or Ninti, the 'Lady of Life' and the wife of Enki, the 'Lord of the Earth' whose water fertilized her. Ninti was an earth goddess known as the 'Lady of the Great Mountain' and was associated with the stony margins of the desert where the ground could be made fertile. Her emblem was the cow because she nourished the kings of Sumer with her milk giving them the divinity and authority to govern the kingdom for the gods.

Both the Euphrates and Tigris have their source in the snow-capped mountains in eastern Anatolia and represented the streaming tears of the mother goddess, Tiamat. The Euphrates was seen as the 'River of Creation' but was also associated with the 'River of the Night' and was seen as the 'River of Huber' or the 'River of the Underworld' that was governed by the water demon Tiamat. Her upper half governed the waters of the subterranean ocean and her lower half reigned over the terrestrial waters of the Euphrates.

The capital city of Sumer was Ur, the home of magic and astrology and under the rule of Sin, the Moon God, who governed the other gods and goddesses. Other city-states flourished in Sumer, each designed the same to house the human labour force to build the city and work the farms. Fired mud bricks were used to construct protective city walls, houses, workshops, gardens and parks that surrounded the most important building of them all, the temples, called ziggurats, stepped pyramids that honoured a local Anunnaki god or goddess at the centre dominating the city.

The Sumerian architects placed great emphasis on the temple, seeing it as the 'House of the Abyss' because its foundations were sunk deep within the ancient waters of Tiamat with the temple pillars reaching the underworld attaching the realm of Ereshkigal to the earth and sky realms of Ishtar, in a sense connecting death to life. For a temple to work it had to convince the population that the heavenly deity was actually present within its walls watching over the city and keeping its inhabitants safe. It was in the temple the gods shared their knowledge with humanity through the priests. The earthly temple was an exact copy of the heavenly temple of the gods, which could have worked like a star gate, a portal that allowed the gods and goddesses to interact with humans.

A breakaway group of priest kings migrated westwards towards the setting sun settling in Egypt beside the River Nile as the First Dynasty of pharaohs in 3100BCE. They bought with them the Father Osiris, the Son Horus and the holy spirit of Isis.

The Sumerian priests put on 'mystery plays' each year at the temple dedication feast and New Year festivals re-enacting the epic creation story between Marduk played by the king and the she dragon, Tiamat, by a high priestess. Ritual was seen as the process through which the temple functioned as a means of communication with the other worlds.

Craftsmen made beautiful jewellery made from gold and silver with inlaid precious stones like lapis lazuli and jade that would adorn the gods and goddess and kings and queens, princes and princesses. The Sumerians produced the first coloured pottery, made the first musical instruments and developed the first written language. They used a system of counting and writing to record transactions and set laws. They spoke an agglutinative tongue, a synthetic language using simple roots of words alongside hand signals and facial expressions. Scribes, highly trained family members of the priests, wrote on clay tablets using sharpened reed stalks to create shaped characters. As well as record keeping and laying down the law, the tablets were used for retelling the epic tales of their gods and goddesses, kings and heroes fighting an endless battle against the demonic forces that lurked in the chaos of darkness.

Young Ishtar

Ishtar and Ereshkigal both had leading roles in many of the sagas preserved on the clay tablets giving us plenty of information on their antics. The earlier Sumerian tablets called Ishtar, Inanna who was the world's first goddess of love and also the original resurrection. Inanna liked the finer things in life, flowing gossamer dresses, delicate rich scents, the most expensive jewellery, the finest make-up and the best haircut. She loved life and all the pleasures that it offered whereas Ereshkigal loathed it, she knew it was all an illusion. It was a false world with the indigenous race subject to Anunnaki rule, being influenced to spend a lifetime paying taxes and making sacrifices so that their masters, the priests and kings could grow fat, wealthy and powerful like the gods they served. Ereshkigal pitied the human race, treated badly and put to work like the cattle, to farm, build, weave, bake and fish in return for shelter, food and protection from the dark forces that wandered in the desert. The talented human could become artists, musicians, entertainers or wrestlers rising up through the Sumerian hierarchy in search for wealth and status.

Inanna and Ereshkigal were born from the Moon God Sin, whom the Sumerians called Nanna who was the son of the God of Air, Enlil, the half-brother of Enki, and the grain goddess Ninlil. Enlil, the son of Anu, Heaven, and Ki, Earth, was banished to the underworld for raping the grain goddess. Being pregnant with his child, Ninlil refused to leave his side and accompanied Enlil to the world of death and darkness. Rather than allowing Nanna to be born in the dark confines of the underworld, Ninlil was permitted to leave so that the Moon could journey through the night sky in a circular ship accompanied by the stars and planets on the promise that the first born of the Moon God would be delivered to the underworld in order to rule over it.

Sometime later the Queen of Heaven, Inanna, felt it was her time to be Queen of the underworld too, so planned a journey to visit her sister Ereshkigal in her dark gloomy realm. Inanna instructed her adviser that if she did not return in three days, he was to perform mourning rites for her then go to the three high gods in turn, Enlil of Nippur, Nanna of Ur and Enki of Eridu and implore them to intervene on her behalf so that she will not die in the underworld. Inanna is dressed in her best royal apparel and her most expensive jewellery when she arrives at the gate of the underworld to be challenged by the gatekeeper of the seven gates. He informs Inanna that by the orders of Ereshkigal and in accordance with the laws of the underworld the goddess of love must remove a piece of attire or adornment at each of the gates as she descends deeper into the earth. Inanna passes through the seventh gate naked to face her sister and the seven Anunnaki judges. They turn their gaze on Inanna who dies immediately and her corpse is hung unceremoniously on a stake. When his queen does not return after three days the adviser does as instructed and after performing the mourning rites for her, he contacts the three high gods in turn. Enlil and Nanna refuse to intervene but Enki creates two golems from the dirt beneath his fingernails and sends them to the realm of Ereshkigal with the food and water of life. They sprinkle the food and water of life over the corpse of Inanna sixty times and the goddess is restored to life. A law of the underworld is that no one can leave without providing a replacement so two demons accompany Inanna to the land of the living to carry back the substitute to the underworld. When she reached Erech, her own city she finds her husband Dumuzi, the god of vegetation, partying and having too much of a good time in her absence and is incensed. She hands Dumuzi over to the demons to take her place in the land of the dead. With the god of vegetation gone from the land nature begins to die so Utu the Sun God turned Dumuzi into a snake so he could escape up through the cracks in the rock to the surface and restore order to the land.

Before Sumer

As we have seen, the Sumerian civilization migrated south from what is now Turkey to build the first civilisation around 7,500 years ago. They originated from close to the source of the Euphrates and Tigris Rivers near to a Neolithic temple shrine discovered in 1995 with over three quarters still to be excavated to date called the Göbekti Tepe. This ancient site, situated close to what is today the border of war torn Syria and Iraq, has been designated the oldest temple in the world constructed around 9,500BCE. Göbekti Tepe which means 'hill of the navel' or 'hill of the sacred centre' was managed by a priestly race dressed in vulture feathers who practiced rituals and ceremonies at the subterranean site. A series of T-shaped pillars around ten feet tall and weighing approximately fifty tons each were orientated roughly north to south and carved with high relief depictions of animals that held up a simple roof. The underground shrines were entered by stone portals in the roof and south facing doorways. There is no evidence of human habitation which suggests the shrine was purely a ceremonial centre. Around 7,500BCE after 2,000 years of use Göbekti Tepe was deliberately filled in and abandoned for some unknown reason.

Within a thirty mile radius a number of Neolithic shrines that were in use around the same time as Göbekti Tepe have recently been discovered. At Karaham Tepe in the Teklek Mountains a number of T-shaped pillars similar to those at Göbekti Tepe have been unearthed, most aligned north to south in rows and in pairs with similar carvings on them. Amongst the weather worn pillars worked flint tools have been found everywhere over the site. Many of the standing stones face towards the midsummer sunrise. Nearby at Sogmatar the remains of seven temples, each thought to represent one of the celestial bodies that circle the earth have been discovered. Another recent discovery at Cayonu

Tepesi the shrine temples are orientated north to south have been dated to have been in use between 7,300 and 5,900BCE.

Five hundred miles to the west on the fertile plains of central Turkey is Çatal Hüyük, discovered in 1959, it was a farming community in use between 7,000 and 5,500BCE. This settlement consisted of tightly packed houses constructed of mud brick and plaster built around small courtyards. Surrounding the settlement crops of wheat, barley, lentils and peas were cultivated. It was an agricultural community that lived a peaceful existence where a third of the structures were used as religious shrines venerating the goddess. It was the ability of the goddess, the feminine energy of the universe, that gave her fertility ensuring enough crops and fruit grew every season to sustain the whole community throughout the entire year.

Around fifty pregnant female figurines made from terracotta, chalk, alabaster, marble, limestone and volcanic rock have been unearthed from around the site. A terracotta figure of the Mother Goddess giving birth on her throne between two leopards was found in a grain bin. One goddess statue discovered had a single body with a single pair of arms but had two heads and two sets of breasts, perhaps a prototype for Ishtar and Ereshkigal, reflecting the twin aspects of a single body of the feminine force.

Skulls of vultures were found protruding from the walls of the shrines. They were covered with plaster with the tips of the beaks forming nipples suggesting nourishment and new life. The role of the vulture in Neolithic Turkey was to accompany the dead to the afterlife in the north and to bring fresh souls back to be born into newly born babies.

11,000 years ago the North Star was in the constellation of the vulture, known today as Cygnus. It was seen as the realm of the underworld and was the destination of the feather clad shaman to commune with the ancestors. North was the direction of the primal cause, or the 'world axis', the point in the heavens around which the Earth and the stars revolve. It was the umbilical cord from which our planet receives nourishment from the source of creation and the manifestation of the Goddess herself. It is from where the seven rays of existence emanate to become the divine laws from which the gods and goddesses and the human soul are born and contains the dormant matter that contains the four basic elements.

The dead were left exposed to the elements to be picked clean by vultures before being wrapped in cloth, animal skins or matting, bound with cord and placed within the home below the storage and bed platforms. The rooms had a central hearth and an oven, upper living quarters and storage spaces. The walls were decorated with sophisticated paintings portraying animals, goddesses and abstract patterns and shapes. According to Karen Tate in her book 'Sacred Places of Goddess', the imagery on the walls depicted the close connection between the mother, the daughter and the son represented by the bull as their consort. Vultures painted on the walls in red hovering over headless people in the embrace of their wings is seen by archaeologists as representing the goddess of death and rebirth. Bull's heads appear on the walls of one chamber that is believed to be a birthing room. The horns represent the regenerative powers of the goddess.

Çatal Hüyük was abandoned around 5,500BCE due to climate change with rising temperatures melting the retreating ice sheets of the northern hemisphere causing global flooding and the need to expand with a growing population unable to spread out across the mountainous regions of Turkey. They would have been aware of the life giving rivers of the Euphrates and Tigris and the open spaces that Mesopotamia offered for a large and ever growing population to thrive. Slowly these people led by the priests migrated into the Mesopotamian desert gaining knowledge of the land to be able to construct large city states to contain the large populations. With the cities came hierarchies and manmade laws to ensure safe and manageable societies.

The Rise of Babylon

Sumer thrived for a thousand years until a force swept down from the north around 2,300BCE to take over the control of the region between the Euphrates and the Tigris known as Mesopotamia, literally 'between the rivers'. Great armies led by a king from Akkad arrived on chariots wearing bronze helmets and armour to rule over an empire that stretched from Syria in the north and the Persian Gulf in the south. This mighty conquering force was led by the Akkadian king Sargon the Great who made Babylon his central powerbase from which to govern the empire. He built Babylon, or 'babilan', which means 'Gate of the Gods' on the banks of the River Euphrates 150 miles upstream from the old capital of Ur. The city-state had magnificent temples and palaces. Winding roads were lined with houses, parks and gardens surrounded by a massive fortified wall made from mud fired bricks and decorated with coloured glazed tiles. Giant gates and tall towers finished off the city wall which not only protected the community but also symbolised great wealth and power to any outsider. The city was built on the banks of the Euphrates, one-half on each side and by the time of King Hammurabi in 1736BCE was possibly the largest city the world had ever seen. Hammurabi introduced laws that applied across the whole of his empire covering family, criminal and civil matters, most punishable by death if transgressed. Trade was no longer controlled by the state as merchants had become wealthy and in a position to manage themselves. Laws were recorded so the king could have some control over the corporations including 'the strong shall not injure the weak' to protect the lower working classes. A system of set prices, wages and a tax system was put in place to encourage the population to support the cause of God and King.

The first Babylonian king, Sargon, so the cuneiform texts

tell us had a human mother who became pregnant when an Anunnaki god forced himself on her. To protect her son when he was born from persecution and ridicule for being conceived out of wedlock, he was hidden in a wicker basket and floated down the Euphrates. The child was found and raised by a royal servant of the king of Kish where he quickly rose through the ranks to become the king's cup bearer, an officer of high rank whose duty was to serve drinks at the royal table. From there Sargon, probably through marriage, became the king of Akkad.

The new rulers over the Mesopotamian people adopted the old Sumerian culture, their ways and their gods and goddesses. They changed the names of the deities of the trinity; Nanna became the Moon God Sin, Utu, the Sun God Shamash and the Queen of Heaven, Inanna became the Star of Heaven, Ishtar.

The conquest led to a group of Sumerian priest kings migrating south eastwards into the fertile seasonal flooding Indus valley. The Babylonian empire also made use of the Sumerian cuneiform writing for their record keeping, their laws and storytelling. The Akkadians also introduced a new language to the Mesopotamian region, a Semitic tongue that used coherent sentences allowing a deeper meaning to conversations and ideas; a language with imagination. The first poetry was born and songs with heart performed. Saragon made one of his daughters, Enheduanna, a priestess of the Moon God Sin at Ur. She is believed to be the world's oldest known poet with her 'Great Above to the Great Below' also translated as 'From the Sky to the Land of the Dead' which tells of the journey the love goddess made into the underworld realm to confront her sister and endure death.

The old Sumerian myths were embellished with detail and creative description to enhance a new generation of god and goddess worshippers who worked to keep the Babylonian empire thriving. A new creation myth was revealed that made the chief fertility god of Babylon, Marduk, the biblical Moloch, into the king over the other gods and goddesses and the Moon

God Sin demoted to a general in his army. The myth also reveals that, to become king, Marduk had defeated Tiamat.

The Original Mother

The Babylonian creation myth is revealed on six clay tablets discovered in Nineveh on the Tigris River and translated in 1876. It confirms the divine authority given to Marduk, allowing him to guide the destiny of the world to his will. The tablets take us back to the beginning of time when all that existed was the fresh waters of Apsu and a salt water ocean called Tiamat. Tiamat, which means 'Mother of Life' is described as a boundless ocean of salt water floating in nothingness, asleep. She was slowly stirred awake by the presence of the fresh rain and river waters of Apsu. An attraction pulled them together to merge and give birth to the universe starting with the god of chaos Mummu, who was the waves that stirred the waters into action and change. Mummu was an immense energy that contained all the elements that the physical universe is made of. Apsu, the father and the source of all knowledge and wisdom circled and supported the Earth, spreading happiness and abundance across the planet. Next came the twin brothers Lahmu and Lahamu (Mars and Venus), described as the silt deposits found at the edge of the water line. Then came Anshar and Kishar (Saturn and Jupiter) described as the gods of the circular horizon between the sky and the Earth followed by the sky god Anu and the water god Enki, the great sorcerer and the source of all magic.

The gods enjoyed the pleasures that paradise had to offer, like partying, lovemaking and exploration on the fertile planet of Earth making a constant racket that soon began to disturb Tiamat and Apsu. It was not long before they could both stand it no longer. They plotted with Mummu how to best deal with their noisy offspring. Apsu and Mummu wanted to destroy them all with floodwaters but Tiamat was reluctant to do so, she did not want to kill her children. While they argued, Enki got wind of the plotting and decided to act first before his parents could put their plan into action. Using a powerful spell, Enki puts Apsu into a deep sleep, binds Mummu to him and imprisons them both in a sacred chamber deep underground. Enki, the Lord of the Earth then takes control of the fresh subterranean waters of his father for his own use. Tiamat is stirred into action by her other children to take revenge on the noisy gods for the death of her husband and firstborn. She gives birth to an army of demons to follow her son Kingu, the Moon into battle against the younger gods passing onto him the 'Tablets of Destiny' to ensure victory.

During a council of the gods, Enki's son Marduk agrees to lead an army against Tiamat but only on the condition that he is given full authority over the gods and could determine the destiny of the Earth. The council agree to his terms and crown him king. To prove that he has the power to carry out his promise, Marduk makes his royal robe disappear in front of the assembly and make it appear again. The gods were satisfied and proclaimed him King of the Gods, King of the solar system and King of the whole universe. Marduk prepares for battle by arming himself with a bow and arrows, a mace, a rod of lightning and a net held at the corners by the four winds. He then fills his body with fire, creates seven raging hurricanes, mounts his flying storm chariot and feeling confident, races towards the advancing Tiamat with his own and the Earth's destiny in his hands.

Coming face to face with the 'she dragon', an enemy of the state, a dangerous terrorist, the Babylonian hero challenges Tiamat to single combat, to which she agrees. The two divine opposing armies encircle the Mother Goddess and the King of the Gods posturing towards each other, chanting and name calling. Marduk is the first to move, casting his net in Tiamat's direction who retaliates by flying forward opening her mouth to swallow her grandson. Marduk dives out of her way unleashing an evil wind into her mouth inflating her body like a balloon and lets fly an arrow into her swollen belly causing her heart to split in two and die.

The Goddess was dead; long live the God. This was the moment when the balance of the universe began to favour the masculine power and women became under the influence of men. Tiamat's demons turn to flee but are caught up in Marduk's net, rounded up and bound tight. Marduk takes the Tablets of Destiny from Kingu and places them onto his own chest; now he ruled the universe. With Tiamat slain in front of him, Marduk cuts her body in two, making the bottom half of her into the Earth and her top half exiled to the furthest reaches of the heavens in a guarded prison under orders to not let the water of the Mother Goddess to escape.

With the Tablets of Destiny safely hung around his neck Marduk proceeds to record his story. He first organises the universe by introducing a calendar establishing the course of the year based on the changing cycle of the sun rather than the moon. Time was divided into parts that followed a straight path from a past to the present where it would continue to advance into the future for eternity. Gone were the old ways of the natural rhythm of birth, growth, decay, death and rebirth nature of the feminine force, a spiral of learning and experience in search for knowledge and wisdom. To crown things off, Marduk puts the mighty planet Jupiter in charge of the celestial order. Sin was demoted to a general; Ishtar was awarded the throne of heaven and access to the higher self of Tiamat while Ereshkigal was sent to rule the realm of the dead deep in the Earth and abode of the lower self of the Mother Goddess.

The cuneiform texts reveal that Marduk made plans to create a human-being to serve and wait on the Anunnaki masters. The rebel leader Kingu was sacrificed and his blood used to fashion the earth beings he required to keep the gods in food and wine. Humanity would build the temples and cities, they would farm the land, bake the bread and weave wool to feed and clothe themselves, the army, the priests, kings and the gods. Finally, Marduk has the greatest temple ever built in the centre of his mighty Babylon.

The influence of Tiamat that had blazed her feminine force for hundreds of thousands of years was fractured into many parts becoming many separate sparks of her authority; lesser goddesses much weaker than any of the gods that now ruled heaven. As individuals they can be kept firmly in place at the kitchen sink and in the bedroom for the pleasure of the gods, kings and heroes.

Ishtar sat on the throne of heaven that existed outside of space and time in the world of spirit. As the Queen of Heaven, Ishtar has the power of the higher energy of Tiamat while her sister Ereshkigal, the Queen of the Dead received the throne of the underworld and the power of the lower energy from the defeated Mother of Life.

For the past 5,000 years or so most of humanity has been guided by the patriarchal God of fear, or more accurately the fear of God. We have been conditioned to fear the unknown, to fear being different to everyone else, the fear of being your true self. It is the fear of making a mistake or of failing, it is the fear of loss and the fear of death but most of all it is the fear of fear itself that plagues our way along our path towards wisdom.

Countries and societies grow like a living cell by dividing itself and moving further from the unity of the universe. This allows the minority to influence and control the herd mind of the masses. We are a society divided by politics, religion, gender, class and sport to name a few of the distractions that keep the truth hidden. Humanity has become so divided that we tend to look for answers inside of us to deal with our outside reality rather than seek outwardly for what we have in common with each other. We all share the same planet, our celestial home that sustain and nourishes us. We all use a physical body to interact with our world and our soul spirit to drive us to success in what we choose to do. Everyone has to breathe the same air, to a degree. We are all born with a need to eat, drink and sleep, we grow, we bleed, we learn and we work and play. We breed and we protect those that we love. We laugh and we cry and ultimately we will die. Sometimes it is good to remember that we are all brothers and sisters of Family Earth.

Daughters of Sin

I have a sister, Lyn. She is two years younger than me and as a big brother I have always done my best to protect her. We have had our fall outs when we were growing up but now we are both in our fifties we are the best of friends. Of course it is a different dynamic to sisters and I see that in Lyn's two daughters, my late mother and my auntie and her two daughters. The best word I can come up with to describe their relationship to each other is competitive. Like all siblings they fall out but most rise above it and make up. There is a special bond between sisters, I see that in my mother and auntie, my cousins and nieces; they share their secrets and clothes and they will stand up for each other when one is threatened or in trouble.

Ishtar and Ereshkigal are not your average sisters. They are the powerful opposing forces of life and death. There is no life without death and there is no death without life. Like light needs the dark to be able to shine, Ishtar needs Ereshkigal to be able to bring love into the world. With their brother and Ishtar's twin Shamash they ensure that nature is fertilized and healthy in a cycle of continued life through the destruction of the old making way for rebirth and transformation.

The Babylonian texts say Ishtar was beautiful and as the goddess of love she had to be. Her vulva is described as the boat of heaven and a fallow field waiting for the plough; raunchy stuff even for the 21st Century. She was the world's first pin up girl. All the gods, kings, heroes and mortal men wanted to sleep with her despite being aware that if they did they would die immediately afterwards. When Ishtar had been fulfilled she would bathe away the smell of sex in a magic lake that would restore her virginity and keep her body young. By all accounts Ishtar had a ferocious sexual appetite and loved to sleep around despite being married to the god of crops and vegetation, Tammuz, whom she loved more than anything else in the world. At the same time Ishtar was also keeping her sister busy with a constant flow of disembodied souls arriving at her realm. Tammuz was the youngest son of Enki and half-brother to Marduk and would die each year at the autumn harvest and rise again with the rebirth of nature in the spring. When he returned to the land of the living he guarded the gate of the sky god, Anu, with his brother, Ningizzida. A red carpet of wild anemones bloomed at the foothills on the desert plains after the winter rains had subsided and seen to represent the blood of Tammuz at his arrival from the underworld at the start of the season of parched earth and withered vegetation. Tammuz became a cult figure in Greece as Adonis, where women venerated him at an annual seven day festival that included loud wailing and self-laceration.

Ishtar journeyed to and from her heavenly home in her 'boat of heaven', a sky ship that flew across the earth like a bird. She would often arrive from the upper world of the heavens into the world of constant change in search of old and new pleasures and excitement. She partied with gods and kings living the life of a goddess of love. Ishtar had a ferocious temper and was not a goddess to be messed with. She was strong willed and her most powerful weapon was her fierce threatening tongue but she had a vulnerable side as well. Ishtar had taken a young huluppu tree, what experts believe to be a palm tree, from the banks of the Euphrates and replanted it in her garden. She wanted to make a bed and a throne from its timber when it had matured. When the tree was ready to chop down Ishtar found that a serpent had made its nest in the roots and a vulture with its young roosted in its branches and both had refused to move. The king of Erech, Gilgamesh, came to Ishtar's aid and removed the snake and the bird for her. In gratitude Ishtar gave him a magic drum and drumstick made from the base and crown of the tree.

It is worth mentioning another story concerning a bird of prey, a serpent and a tree revealed on a copper cylindrical seal.

An eagle and a serpent swore a solemn oath of friendship to look after and protect each other's young when they were away hunting. The eagle nested in the tall branches while the serpent and his young lived amongst the exposed roots at its base. For a time this arrangement worked well until one day while the serpent was away searching for food, the eagle pounced on his young and fed them to his own.

Finding his home destroyed and his babies gone, the serpent appeals to Shamash for revenge over the eagle for breaking their oath of friendship. The sun god revealed to him how to capture the bird, break his wings and leave him to suffer in a deep pit. Here the eagle laid in pain and torment for what seemed like eternity crying to Shamash for help. After he felt that the eagle had served his punishment, Shamash guided Etana, the King of Kish, to come to the rescue of the stricken bird. Etana became the first king of Kish by shepherding a people in chaos and without guidance after the flood. For him to secure the permanence of his kingship, Etana needed an heir to continue his legacy and he had no son. Offering daily sacrifices to Shamash to grant him an heir, the sun god sends the king into the mountains where he would find an injured eagle in a pit. The king is told that if he saves the bird he will be guided to a magic herb that will bring him a son. When Etana comes across the eagle he is promised by the bird that he will bring him the 'plant of birth'. For over two seasons Etana brings food and drink to the eagle until he had regained his strength and as promised carried the king to the throne of Ishtar. In some versions of the story Etana succeeds in his quest and has a son. In others he grows dizzy the higher they got into the heavens and begs the eagle to return to the ground. On the descent the eagle runs out of strength and the two of them crash heavily to the earth. A list of kings recorded on a tablet has the name of Etana's son and successor suggesting that his journey was a successful one.

In a conservation with Bill Moyers, an acclaimed American

television journalist, about the 'Power of Myth' and made into a book, Joseph Campbell reveals that the bird is symbolic of the release of the spirit from bondage to the earth and the serpent is symbolic of the bondage to the earth. The serpent is tied to the earth by gravity and represents all creatures including humans whose consciousness revolves around its physical surroundings. The eagle on the other hand can defy gravity and soar into the heavens like the gods. It represents the spiritual flight the soul can make when untied from the physical body. From the combination of the two we get the dragon, a serpent with eagle wings.

It is not a good idea to refuse the advances of the Queen of Heaven. On one of her visits to Earth, Ishtar falls in love with the strength and beauty of the hero Gilgamesh on his return from slaying an evil fire-breathing giant who guarded the great cedar forest of Enlil in the far north of the Babylonian empire. Gilgamesh rejected her advances knowing that if he became her lover he would die. Enraged by his refusal, Ishtar asks Anu to avenge her by sending the Bull of Heaven to destroy Erech, where Gilgamesh was king. Before the total destruction of the city the sacred bull is killed by Gilgamesh's heaven sent companion Enkidu. Because the bull represented the will of heaven Enkidu is condemned to death and is taken to the realm of Ereshkigal causing Gilgamesh to begin his quest for mortality.

Ereshkigal is a different story; always lurking in the shadows but veiled by darkness in the cuneiform texts. The Queen of the Dead did not much like the human world. She much preferred her isolation in the depths of the earth, enjoying her own company, ruling over ghosts and demons, and the visits of her husband Nergal when he could escape the busy world on the surface. Ereshkigal ventured above ground occasionally with some of her demons to steal away the souls of drunken men after she had satisfied her lust for intercourse. Like her younger sister, Ereshkigal loved passionate sex, finding her prey late at night in taverns and clubs but unlike Ishtar she had no magic lake where she could regain her virginity. Ereshkigal was married to the war god Nergal, another son of Enki and brother to Tammuz and ruler of the planet Mars. He is known to be responsible for civil disorder.

Ishtar was seen as the Morning Star of Venus and was portrayed as the Light Bringer, or Lucifer, becoming male for the patriarchal medieval thought of the rising power of the church in Europe. Her symbol was a serpent wrapped around the Tree of Life. The Evening Star of Venus was Ereshkigal who heralded in the night and darkness, in other words, the Night Bringer. The dark of night was when Ereshkigal would allow her demons to roam free on the earth in search of weak-minded men and women to possess and enjoy the excesses of pleasure that the material world had on offer. Ishtar and Ereshkigal give potency to all women and everything that their feminine essence pervaded. Together they protected all women.

Symbols that represented Ishtar included the pentagram that she wore above her breasts and the swastika that adorned her pubic triangle. The pentagram represents harmony, health and magical power. It originated in Mesopotamia as an astronomical diagram showing the movement of the planet Venus as seen from the earth. The swastika is a positive symbol meaning universal regeneration that represents the cosmic dynamism and creative energy. The word comes from the Sanskrit 'su' which means 'well' and 'asti' meaning being. The swastika is a symbol of the life force and cyclic regeneration of nature.

Two birds whose nature generally represents wisdom, intellect and power of thought become the embodiment of the goddesses. For Ishtar it is the dove, a universal symbol of the divine or Holy Spirit. It was the symbol of peace and love. For Ereshkigal it is the crow, a scavenger and the symbol of war, death and loss. The crow represented the need to move on and a sign of coming change.

Where Ishtar was the embodiment of life, Ereshkigal radiated death where ever she went. Between them they keep the light and dark forces of the universe balanced, never allowing one to overcome the other. Their union allows rebirth to occur, for nature to bloom and for humankind to evolve and transform into a race on a journey towards knowledge and wisdom.

Welcome to Hell

Everyone knows of Hell and most would agree that its realm is deep in the bowels of earth somewhere. It counter balances the realm of Heaven, hidden deep in the universe, somewhere. The balancing point of Hell and Heaven is Earth, our realm of space and time consisting of possibilities and chance driven by emotions and feelings wrapped up in fate and fortune. Our ancestors called Hell the nether world or underworld because it nested beneath the middle realm of our world that we experience through the five senses. Heaven, or the upper world is perched above our world where only the angels can fly.

The belief of an underworld has been in the human consciousness ever since we began to bury our dead with grave goods to accompany the spirit on its journey to continue the next stage of its existence in a sacred space within the womb of the earth. Our Stone Age ancestors understood that at death, the essence of the person is returned to the womb of the goddess and the body fed the worms and birds. Their world was a sacred kingdom governed by earth spirits that lived in trees, hills, rivers, springs and caves. They believed that a spirit lived inside themselves that would return to its source in the womb of Mother Earth deep underground when the body died.

Very little evidence has been discovered describing the realm of Ereshkigal. Very few visitors to Huber have ever returned to tell their tale. One such person, albeit a supernaturally created wild man bought into the world for a challenge to Gilgamesh, journeyed to the Babylonian underworld and was able to reveal a glimpse into the shadowy realm of Ereshkigal. Enkidu arrived as a vibrant force of nature and was friends to all the animals and trees. He became a pest to Gilgamesh's hunters and woodcutters who damaged and killed nature, quickly catching the attention of the King who came to trap the beast. After several failed attempts,

Enkidu is lured to the edge of the forest by the sweet scent of a beautiful woman from the city, employed by Gilgamesh. They make love for seven days and nights after which nature turns its back on the wild man and the forest animals run away from him because he had been tainted by society. He moves into the city with his woman, beats Gilgamesh in a fight and out of respect for each other become great friends going on many adventures together. The wild man had been tamed and Gilgamesh had won his challenge. Their bond was so tight that when Gilgamesh's sacred drum and drumstick had somehow managed to find itself into the realm of Ereshkigal, Enkidu offered to go down and retrieve it for him. Inside her gates he is captured and held prisoner. Gilgamesh appeals to the gods for help and Enki orders Nergal to make a hole in the ground so Enkidu's spirit could escape back to the surface. On his return he reveals to Gilgamesh how he saw his body devoured by vermin and filled with dust. He noticed too that those that had received proper funeral rites lived in paradise and those that did not had to make do with a miserable existence. A great advert for the priests who had written the myths.

After many years and more heroic adventures with his great companion, Gilgamesh, it was time for Enkidu to return to the world of the dead. On his deathbed after slaying the Bull of Heaven, Enkidu whispers to Gilgamesh of a dream he had of the underworld.

The God of Death transformed me so my arms were like those of a bird. Looking at me, Nergal leads me along the road from which there is no way back, towards the 'House of Darkness' and abode of Ereshkigal'. I came to the house which none leave who enter, wherein the dwellers are bereft of light, where dust is their fare and clay their food, all residing in darkness. They are clothed like birds with wings for garments.

Rivalling Babylon in wealth and power at the time was the Harappan Indus Valley culture and the Egyptians. Both had upper and middle realms and also a mysterious underworld for the dead to reside in after death.

The deities if the Indus Valley civilisation are unknown, as their script has never been translated. A handful of priest king statuettes have been found at Harappa in the north and Mohenjo Daro in the south reveals a religion that involved city gods at the top of a hierarchy. By the time of the epic sagas of the Vedas, around 1,500BCE the underworld ruler of the Indus Valley was the green skinned Yama. Sacred Indian texts reveal that Yama was the first man to journey to the underworld of the ghosts and return safely back to the land of the living. Because he discovered the path that led to the otherworld, death was introduced into the world to discourage other mortals to search for the secret path.

For the people who settled along the Indus valley when the soul leaves the body it has to cross the mighty River Vaitarani to reach the judgement room. The earthly deeds of the soul are read out to Yama who chooses whether to send it to the realm of twenty one hells or back to the world of humanity for rebirth. During their journey to the land of the dead, the souls become bathed in a lustre like that of the gods before arriving to join the ancestors living in a bliss with Yama. They will sit in the shining paradise alongside the celestial deities forever. Yama had the power to prolong life of a dying person on condition that another individual gave up part of their life to compensate. He might also agree to restore a soul to its body in response to a mortal appeal for someone who had attained great sacredness.

It sounds like a paradise, all light and fluffy compared to Ereshkigal's realm of dust and vermin; unless you receive a proper priestly funeral of course. The Egyptian underworld was different again, for them it was a realm of nightmares. Hieroglyphs found engraved onto a temple wall tells of the emergence from the primeval waters of Nun, the 'Island of the Egg', the creative force responsible for the formation of the earth. Egg Island became a tomb for the first divine inhabitants and was recognised as being the first resting place of green skinned Osiris, the Lord of Death. At the edge of the water that surrounded the island in a field of reeds was a sacred realm called Wetjeset-Neter where sixty posts served as perches for the early gods. These divine beings were led by a group that assumed the form of falcons calling themselves the Sages, who worked for the mysterious figure called 'This One' whose face shone like the sun and had the form of a bird. A serpent known as the 'Great Leaping One' was opposed to the nest of This One and his Sages and a war broke out between them. The birdmen had a weapon called the 'Sound Eye' that somehow caused the destruction of the island which sinks beneath the sea once more.

After some time the island returns from beneath the Nun as the 'Underworld of the Soul'. This second generation of divine inhabitants of the island were known as the 'Lords of the Island of Trampling; and had names like, 'the Far Distant', the Mariner', 'the Lord of the Perch' and 'the Winged Ones'. They were living and breathing gods on earth.

The underworld was the night realm of the Sun God Ra. Once he had set on the western horizon Ra begins a complex journey through the underground world of Osiris in darkness known as the duat which is divided into twelve equal parts. Ra is pulled along in a high prowed boat crewed by lesser deities through each division of night where a different challenge awaits the Sun God in each. Ra has to avoid ghosts and demons, pits of fire, stabbing knives, streams of boiling water, foul smells and fiery serpents before he can return above at sunrise to begin a fresh day. After all twelve divisions had been successfully completed the sun would be reborn at dawn on the eastern horizon.

For a disembodied soul to enter the underworld they sought permission from Osiris who would decide their fate after the jackal headed Anubis balanced the heart against the feather of truth. The Ibis headed scribe, Thoth, recorded the result in his book of the dead. Thoth was strongly compared to the Babylonian god Ningishzidda and was one of the gods of the first time alongside Osiris and taught humanity language, mathematics, geometry, music and art. He enscribed twelve keys on emerald tablets that reveal the secrets of the gods for a select elite order on earth. One tablet reveals that deep in the heart of the earth lie three halls; the 'Halls of Amenti' for the immortals, the 'Halls of the Living', which bathed in the fire of the infinite all and the 'Halls of the Dead' for disembodied souls.

The Halls of Amenti was filled with life and light from above for the thirty-two who came to reside where the river of life flows eternally in the womb of Mother Earth. The great hall was shielded from the darkness of death for the thirty-two to live for eternity. Deep in the Halls of the Living grew a flower of fire that drove away the forces of night around which the thirty-two Children of Light sat on thrones that surrounded the divine flower, bathing in the radiance of eternal light; the spirit of life. Seated within the flower of radiance sat Seven Lords from the world of space and time directing the destiny of humanity with the Children of Light. The Seven Lords rule forever with infinite wisdom and are bound and yet not bound to the dark Halls of Death. The Seven originated from beyond space and time, formed from the order of all and from a place of infinite end when humanity were without form, though the Seven too were once men. Great is the wisdom of the Seven, found hidden in the darkness who shine when lit by the flame of the soul. They are One with the soul of our time.

Revealed on Tablet 2, 'Hall of Amenti', Thoth records his guided tour of the underworld (my wording).

I was led through the dark passages of the Hall of Death into a hall where the Dark Lord sat shrouded in darkness and yet filled with light at the same time. Before me there arose a great throne of darkness on which a figure of the darkest night sat. The dark figure raised its hand from which a flame sprang, growing clear and bright, rolling back the curtain of darkness and lighting the great space of the hall where flame after flame leapt around me. Each flame was surrounded by a shadow of darkness but its light could never be extinguished. The dark figure explained to me that the lights were the souls of men, growing and fading but existing forever, changing, yet living through death into life, growing steady ever upwards into the night. The dark figure concludes by reminding me that death comes to every living thing, yet eternal life exists for all. Then I am led through many halls filled with mysteries that humankind may never know until they too are a Sun of the Light. The gateway to life is through death, not as we know death but a death that is life and fire.

A person is a star that is bound to a body until it is freed from the struggle on earth by the death of the body. All that exists is only another form of that which does not yet exist as everything passes into another being at the end of its life.

Throughout the tablets Thoth reminds humanity that they will remain forever in darkness if they are not aware that the true light is from within. When the soul moves on at death it leaves behind the darkness of night and is free from the toils of oppression. From out of the darkness the soul ascends to be one with the light of the stars. Those that know that the fire is within will ascend into the eternal fire and bathe in it forever. The inner flame is the most potent force in the universe for it overcomes all things and penetrates everything on earth. Know that darkness and light are both of one nature; two sides of the same coin, for each arose from the source of all. Darkness is the chaos of change and Light is order from change. Darkness transformed is the light of the light or the son of the sun.

Into the Underworld (again)

Despite being unfaithful to her husband on numerous occasions, Ishtar loved Tammuz. Marriage was seen very differently five and a half thousand years ago to how we see it today. Of course love mattered but it was not the love we understand today, an individual love between two people where the stomach churns and the heart flutters. Love was not an emotion but a commitment to your partner through respect for your father and the family. It was the father who arranged partners for his children so that the arrangement would benefit his family; his legacy for the future. Making love outside the marriage was not considered unfaithful or even unusual, it was a natural biological urge that needed quenching as you would thirst or hunger. Kings had harems to expand the royal household but he still loved his queen who had to remain faithful, as did the harem, to guarantee true royal heirs. Husbands had mistresses for the pleasure of sex, saving his love for his wife who was chosen for him by his father. Prostitutes had a sacred purpose when giving themselves to men who would donate an offering to the temple for the privilege. The early Christian church recognised that without spiritual love in marriage it would have no meaning in the eyes of God. Marriage had to have a religious significance where the heart would open up to another becoming sick with love and the agony and ecstasy that goes with love.

Love is between two people whatever their status, colour or gender and with love comes loyalty and honesty, trust and forgiveness. The two become one flesh, sacrificing not to each other but to the unity in marriage. It is a sacrifice of the ego to a relationship where two have become one. This was the pledge that Ishtar and Tammuz made to each other on their wedding day. When death came calling taking Tammuz into the depths of Ereshkigal, Ishtar was out of her mind with grief at the loss of half of her soul and half of her whole existence. With grief comes sadness and anger for not being able to do anything about it. Any loss is unfair and unbearable for anyone at any time. As the Queen of Heaven, the daughter of the Moon and sister of the Sun, Ishtar felt that she had a right to have a say in her husband's death. None of the gods on the council wanted to get between Ishtar and Ereshkigal, this was between the two sisters, and they had to sort it out between themselves.

Once Ishtar had made up her mind, there was no changing it; even if it meant manipulating the laws of the universe if she had to, she was going to bring her husband back. Ishtar made an appointment to visit the netherworld of her sister and no god was going to stand in her way and made the preparations to see Ereshkigal in her shadowy world of the dead. First she has to pass successfully through the seven gated walls that separate the living and the dead worlds. Seven great impenetrable walls surrounded Ereshkigal's domain each with tall solid gates guarded by sentries who were fussy who they let in.

Ishtar had to prepare for her seven stages of descent in accordance to the laws of the underworld, a symbolic peeling away of the trappings of life, the status symbols of office until she was free of all her worldly attachments both physically and spiritually that tied her to the world of the living. Only then could Ishtar enter the realm of darkness, the world of ghostly spirits and the prison that held her husband.

Ishtar had her attendants fasten her girdle around her waist forcing her to stand upright in a position of authority and enhances the waistline. It also protected the stomach region and served to carry provisions, money, tools and weapons. It symbolises personal fulfilment and offers divine protection.

Feeling comfortable in her girdle, the maids help Ishtar on with her breast plate of gold over her chest. It protected her vital organs from physical attack and the gold reflects her authority over others on Earth.

Next a necklace of earthly power is placed around Ishtar's neck to ward off any spiritual attack and a set of earrings hung each side of her head so she would always be aware of the whispering universe. Then her crown is lowered onto Ishtar's head, identifying, glorifying and authorizing her the chosen one to govern with divine blessing from the universe. The crown has the power of god and the authority of the goddess.

Next Ishtar is helped on with her royal robe that represents transformation and concealment. Underneath a robe a person can change or hide their shape and dress. It veils the whole body under intrigue and mystery. Finally Ishtar is handed her golden staff, or sceptre, her rod of divine authority. It is a symbol of the snake and implies spiritual knowledge with the power to administer justice. Armed with protection, authority and mystery Ishtar is ready for her journey to the underworld to confront Ereshkigal on her own turf.

Like Inanna before her, Ishtar is requested to remove an adornment at each of the gates she encounters.

Wheels on Fire

Before we join Ishtar's descent to the underworld we need to take a look at the seven energy points found along the human spinal cord through which a stream of energy flows activating each power generator, called chakras, that connect above with below. The word chakra is Sanskrit for wheel that spins in relation to the amount of energy within the body's system. Their purpose is to connect the spiritual universe with the physical psyche. The chakras are situated up the spine from its base at the root chakra and connects the spiritual of the body with the earth forces. At the top of the head is the crown chakra that connects the spiritual of the body to the heavens. The body acts as a conduit between the heaven and the earth. The higher up the spine the energy reaches, the higher the vibration of the chakra, drawing up the 'sleeping serpent' or kundalini from her snug nest. Each chakra represents a progressive state of awareness as the snake climbs up the trunk of the skeleton before branching to the edge of the brain to fly in the heavens like a bird.

We know of the chakras from ancient Hindu scripture revealing the religion of the Indian people that migrated from the Indus Valley and the oldest religion still surviving today. What the Indians priests knew you can be sure that the Babylonian priests knew also, with busy trade routes between the two super powers. As well as exotic foodstuff, materials and trinkets, new thought and ideas were exchanged between the merchants and traders. The sacred Hindu scriptures reveal that within every person dwells an inner feminine energy known as the kundalini, a coiled snake asleep at the bottom of the spine waiting to be awakened. The Ayrians called that feminine force Shakti, the Mother Goddess of all life and the source of all the feminine energy in the universe. Shakti was made up of three goddesses, the gentle, loving Parvati, the warrior queen, Durga, and the bloodthirsty goddess of death and destruction Kali. Shakti was the consort or queen to the four armed, snake adorned Shiva who was god of the mind who when not moving the universe with his dancing would be away fighting demons who were a threat to humanity. Like Shakti, Shiva was one of three forces, three different aspects of the masculine energy of the universe; Bramhan who pervades everything as Brahma the creator, Vishnu the preserver and Shiva the destroyer. It was Shiva's duty to destroy in order to continually renew and refresh the universe; he was the change in the world.

When the kundalini is awakened through moments of ecstasy the serpent rises up the spine from the base to the top of the head to connect with Shiva. First, the root chakra at the tail of the spine spins and vibrates awake activating a red aura connecting the soul to the influence of Saturn the guardian planet. Next the sacral chakra of the genitals pulses into life, becoming orange, drawing on the passion of Mars followed by the yellow glow of the adrenal gland chakra in the stomach connecting to the king of planets, the justice of Jupiter. Reaching the heart chakra Shakti is at the half waypoint of her ascent activating the green aura to bathe in the fertile power of the Sun at the heart of our solar system. Then the deep blue energy of the throat chakra is activated connecting to the love of Venus followed by the awakening of the indigo radiating pineal gland or third eye chakra and the influence of the emotional Moon. Finally the serpent power completes her ascension from earth to heaven when she reaches the pituitary gland or crown chakra at the top of the head with violet energy connecting the soul to the messenger planet Mercury. When all the chakras are open the vibration of the soul resonates with everything else in the universe. By arousing the normally sleeping snake to climb up through the body the female energy of Shakti joins with the male energy of Shiva bringing together the union between the goddess, the god and the soul, father, mother and child together in bliss.

For Ishtar to meet with her sister she had to journey in the opposite direction downwards, returning the ecstatic serpent back into her slumber in her realm of darkness.

The Descent

Ishtar is now ready physically to face Ereshkigal and her descent through the seven gates will prepare her mentally and spiritually. She arrives at the outer wall of the underworld determined to release Tammuz from the clutches of her sister. At the first gate the guard asks Ishtar to leave a piece of her adornment behind before he will allow her to continue into the 'Temple of Love', the realm of the fires of the pituitary gland where the union between the opposing forces of heaven and earth come together. It is the sacred hall where the physical you ends and the rest of the universe begins. Here lies the mind. The crown chakra is the total energy of all the other chakras. Its essence is clear vision and the heavenly force of wisdom beyond knowledge, love beyond compassion and existence beyond physical life. By giving her crown to the guard, Ishtar is relinquishing her authority of sovereignty over the people of Babylon. She also leaves behind her sight of heaven and the world above.

At the second gate Ishtar removes her earrings for the guard to pass into the 'House of Spells' and the inner vision of the pineal gland or the third eye chakra, the region of insight and self-mastery of the brain. Here Ishtar becomes deaf to the voice of the universe.

Ishtar removes her necklace at the third gate and portal into the 'Temple of Power' of the throat chakra and realm of communication. It is the spinning wheel of intuition that gives a voice to thoughts and feelings. With the necklace gone, Ishtar loses her spiritual protection to charm away evil spirits and any creative words she might have used remain at this gate.

The forth gate marks the mid-way point of her descent where Ishtar takes off her breastplate to enter the 'Meadow of Delights' into the realm of unconditional love and the heart of compassion. The middle gate is the point where the spiritual and the physical separate. With the breastplate, Ishtar leaves behind the last of her physical protection and her love and compassion is lost with it. Now Ishtar was deep in the earth and closer to the dead lands than her beloved living lands on the surface. Anger and rage were still burning through Ishtar's veins; nothing else mattered to her but to free Tammuz.

Arriving at the 'Secret Valley' in the solar plexus, Ishtar discards her girdle at the fifth gate before entering the realm of controlled emotions through will power. The stomach chakra is where instinct and passion are awakened and establishes the sense of self. Here Ishtar leaves behind her femininity and sexuality at the gate and loses any sense of who she is. All she knew because it was burning in her heart was to rescue her love from death.

At the sixth gate Ishtar enters the 'Garden of Beauty' in the region of the pancreas at the base of the stomach. Here is the realm of physical pleasure and the centre of creativity. The Sacral chakra ensures the harmony in relationships and connections. Handing over her sceptre to the guard Ishtar is giving away her final piece of authority leaving her uncreative and impassionate. Finally, Ishtar arrives at the seventh and final gate naked and unprotected under her robe. Removing her final piece of attire Ishtar reveals her true naked self, her body and looks that men would die for on the surface but it had no impact here. Ishtar was now ready to pass through to the 'Mountain of the Soul' of the root chakra, the realm that connects the invisible to the visible and is the essence of health and vitality. It houses the ancestral tribal vibrations. By leaving her robe behind Ishtar is stripped of her mystery and all connection with the living world has gone.

Ishtar had nothing more to hide and was ready to face Ereshkigal and plead for the release of Tammuz. As she waited for the gatekeeper to open the final gate, Ishtar wastes no time calling out to her sister waiting inside.

> *Oh gatekeeper, open the gate,*
> *Open the gate so that I may enter!*
> *If thou openest not the gate*
> *So that I cannot enter*
> *I will smash the door and shatter the bolt,*
> *I will shatter the doorpost and I will remove the doors.*
> *I will raise up the dead so they can eat the living,*
> *And the dead will outnumber the living.*

Ishtar had threatened the first zombie holocaust to enter the world of the living if she did not get her way. Enraged, Ishtar stormed into the realm of Ereshkigal to face her sister to demand the release of Tammuz but she had not reckoned on the dark queen's evil mood and was struck with the curse of death, extinguishing the spark that gave Ishtar life, stopping her in her tracks, falling to the ground, dead. Ereshkigal did not like her sister much.

As Ishtar lay dead in the realm of Ereshkigal alongside the corpse of Tammuz, the world above became infertile, nature withered, cattle refused to mate and men and women became impotent. When humanity reached the point of starvation, Lord Enki had to intervene, creating a eunuch to charm Ereshkigal to give life back to Ishtar. The queen of darkness was enchanted and agreed to release the queen of heaven from death and return to the land of the living with her husband, Tammuz. Ishtar had won. Nature was restored and the catastrophe averted; new-born cattle soon roamed the fields and children suckled on their mothers breasts once more. Ereshkigal demands a replacement for the couple and after some intense and bitter negotiations with the council of gods, Tammuz was ordered to stay with the goddess of death for six months of the year to restore the balance once more.

The city societies were instructed to honour the goddess and god of nature by the priests, with offerings and sacrifices to ensure the continued fertility of the Earth as the presence of Ishtar and Tammuz could only be guaranteed by the generosity of their worshippers.

The Mysterious Seven

The number seven has been important ever since we have been aware of the seven celestial bodies and their influences. From the seven 'planets' we get the seven days and seven rays, seven Lords and seven phases of creation. There are seven seals and seven angels with trumpets and seven vials of God's wrath to herald in Armageddon. Seven is considered to be the perfect number being the combination of the dynamic number three, the trinity of the spiritual father, mother and child, and the stable four of the physical four main elements, four quarters and directions of the earth and the four seasons of the year. Seven is the combination of three parts spirit to four parts matter.

The Seven Rays

According to ancient sacred Hindu scripture, all there is, is an unknown energy from which worlds are made and where life is born, grows, reproduces and dies. Beyond the point from which this energy emanates there is no time as it contains the past, present and future. There is no flow of development because everything just is. From out of this point comes creation divided into seven levels, ways or rays. The vibrations of each ray transform divine ideas into human ideals. The soul is bought into being as invisible sparks of sacred fire gradually becoming clothed with a flesh and bone body ready to be born into a physical human to experience a physical world of constant changing cycles of light and dark, hot and cold and life and death.

At the start the human spirit is the pure white light of the consciousness of the universe that is both the god and goddess but today known as God. Like a light shining through a prism is split into the seven separate colours of the rainbow, the pure spirit is divided into seven rays of light each with its own personality and planetary ruler, a Lord of Light that works to allow the human mind to be comfortable with the divine soul. The rays, or ways, are not sharply defined but blend into each other at the edges. Every one of us whether we are aware of it or not are influenced to some extent by each of the seven rays depending on our particular stage of evolution and learning.

The first Ray is the Way of Purpose or the Will of the God which aligns the human mind with the true purpose of the universe. Its colour is blue and fuels the expressive throat chakra. It is the Word made manifest on Earth. This ray can influence us to become more understanding and cooperative with others. It can give words of wisdom to help those that need encouragement and support in their struggles with life.

The second Ray is the Way of Love or the Wisdom of God that allows the mind to see the divine in everything it experiences. Its colour is violet and marries the wisdom of the crown chakra to the human consciousness. It can transform personal love into universal love.

The third Ray is the way of Compassion or the Love of God that brings stillness allowing us to connect with our feelings. Its green light powers the forgiveness of the pumping heart chakra. This energy lets us just 'be' and become separate from the ever changing world we are constantly busy with and bathe in the reassurance of universal love.

The fourth Ray is the Way of Harmony and Peace or the Miracle of God that expresses the beauty of the birth, death and rebirth cycles of nature that requires nourishment from the balance of fire and water, air and earth to exist. Its orange light excites the passionate sacral chakra manifesting as the beauty we experience in our lives.

The fifth Ray is the Way of Knowledge or the Truth of God that balances the head with the heart. Its colour is purple and is the inner vision of the perceptive pineal gland chakra. This ray lights the path beyond the confines of the mind.

The sixth Ray is the Way of Devotion or the Law of God and is the portal between the higher mind of the invisible and the lower mind of the physical. The yellow light drives the confidence of the solar plexus chakra to deal with both positive and negative emotions that can disrupt the mind from going about its earthly work.

The seventh Ray is the Way of Magick or the Knowledge of God that transforms order from chaos. It is the most elemental form of being and the centre of primal fear. The red light ignites the instinctive root chakra that dances to the rhythm and cycles of the natural world in harmony with the heartbeat of Mother Earth.

The Seven Rays, like the concept of the chakras, is a Hindu awareness of the universe and made popular in the Europe and America by the Ukrainian Madam Blavatsky who founded the Theosophical Society in New York in 1875. Her ideas migrated into Europe by Alice Bailey who channelled an entity she called the Tibetan and founded the Arcane Esoteric School during the early part of the 20th Century which quickly became an alternative to the men only Masonic Society that sought the guidance of a 'Creator' that was purely male.

The Seven Lords

The Seven Lords of Amenti, or Humanity, were Anunnaki gods that resided deep underground in the Halls of the Living within the sacred flower of eternal light.

The first Lord holds the key to all hidden magic and is the creator of the halls of the Dead. His number is THREE from which an energy flows that is shrouded with a darkness that binds the human soul to the physical realm.

The second Lord bestows the power of life to humanity. His body is light and fire and his number is FOUR. He is the Lord that frees the soul at the death of the body.

Next is the Master whose number is FIVE. He is the Lord of

all magick.

The fourth Lord is SIX, the Lord of Light who removes the darkness of the hidden pathway that leads to rebirth into the kingdom of light.

SEVEN is the fifth Lord and the key to the mastery of time. He is the Lord of the vastness of space.

The sixth Lord follows the progress of humankind. His number is EIGHT and he constantly weighs and balances the heart throughout a person's life.

Finally is NINE, the seventh and most powerful Lord, the father who creates form from out of the formless, order from chaos and is the Lord of the Lords. He is the 'Veiled Presence' and is free from space and time. NINE is infinity.

Their wisdom is great and can be found in the darkness when lit by the flame of the soul.

The Seven Days of Creation

It is worth mentioning that a day can mean one revolution of the earth to spin on her axis that takes a little over twenty-four hours. It can also mean the period when it isn't night. Seven days and nights equal one week or a quarter of the moons cycle of a little over twenty-eight days, four complete weeks or a 'moonth' or month. It takes just over 365 days for the earth to compete an orbit of the sun, one more day than the thirteen complete moon cycles.

From maximum daylight at the summer solstice of around seventeen hours in Britain, it takes six months to journey to the minimum daytime of about seven hours at the winter solstice. Twice a year at the equinoxes, day and night are equal, balanced at twelve hours apiece. The summer solstices represent south on a compass directly opposite winter solstice in the north. Spring equinox is in the east and the rebirth of light and autumn equinox represents the west and the death of light. Together the four directions cut the world into quarters and the realms of the four elemental powers.

According to Moses who is credited to writing the first five chapters of the Old Testament including Genesis, the earth and everything on it was created in seven days. He tells his audience that God created the heaven and the earth on the first day. The earth was without form and barren and shrouded in a deep darkness until the spirit of god came to reside on the earth saying 'let there be light', and there was light and God saw that his creation was good. Next God divided the light from the dark calling them day and night. When the first night had passed and a new day began, God decreed the completion of his first day. We call this day Sunday after our star for giving light and heat to our sacred planet.

On the second day, God created the sky over the waters of the earth separating the waters under the earth from the waters that were above completing the second day we call Monday after the moon for giving us our earliest calendar and the reflective presence of the sun during the darkness of night.

The following day God gathered the waters under the heavens together in one place so that dry land could appear and called this dry land the earth and the gathered waters he called the sea. Then God gave birth to nature on the dry land at the end of the third day we call Tuesday, or Tir's day after the Norse God of War, Tir or Tyr.

Next God created the planets and the stars in the heavens to divide the day from the night as signs to mark days, months, seasons and years. He put light in the heavens to give his light to the earth at night. God made two great lights, the greater light to rule the day and a lesser light to rule at night thus ending a good day's work for the fourth day we call Wednesday after Wodin or Odin the king of the Norse gods.

On the fifth morning God gave life to creatures in the seas, on the land and in the air and blessed them all with fertility to exist, grow, reproduce, age and die. We call the fifth day Thursday after the Norse thunder god, Thor.

On the sixth day God created humankind in his image, male and female to be fruitful and have domination over all the creatures and beasts that swam, walked, and flew. We know this day of completion as Friday, named after Freya the Norse goddess of love and an incarnation of Ishtar.

God was pleased with his creation and at the end of his final day of work he looked forward to resting and admiring his great work of creation. We call this day of rest Saturday after the god of boundaries and limits, Saturn.

Revelation of Seven

The modern bible begins with the seven days of creation and ends with the apocalyptic epic of Revelation by the prophet John around a hundred years after the death of his saviour Jesus. This ending chapter is littered with sevens beginning with his messages from God to the seven angels of the seven main churches of Asia. John reveals to us that from God who is, who was and who is yet to come, flows seven spirits that take over John's visions on the Lord's day. John hears a voice that sounded like a trumpet speaking behind him, asking him to write down his experience and send them to the seven churches of Asia. Turning, John was aware that among seven gold lamp stands their stood a being wearing a robe that reached to the ground and a gold belt around his chest. His hair was pure white and his eyes blazed with fire, his feet shone like brass, his voice sounded like a roaring waterfall and his face was as bright as the sun. This figure held seven stars in his right hand and a sharp double edged sword came out of his mouth revealing to John that the seven lamp stands are the seven churches and the seven stars are the seven angels of the churches. John was told to write to the seven churches what he is shown.

The first message was to Ephesus offering to those that win victory over sin and heresy will be given the right to eat fruit from the tree of life that grows in the garden of God.

The message to Smyrna was to be faithful to Him even if it means death. By dying a martyr they cannot be hurt by a second death.

John's message to Pergamum is if they turn from worshipping Baal, eating the food offered to the idols and the practise of sexual pleasure, He will give them some of the hidden manna and a white stone bearing their secret name for the Book of the Living.

The message to Thyatira accuses the angel of tolerating that goddess who calls herself the messenger of god. He has given her the time to repent her sins but she has refused to turn away from her immortality. He will throw her onto a bed with her adulterers to suffer terribly and destroy all her followers. Turn away from these evil teachings and He will give you the authority over nations, to rule with an iron rod and to break into pieces any opposition like clay pots. He would also give them the Morning Star.

In the message to Sardis, John tells those that have kept their clothes clean that they will walk with Him, clothed in white to show they are worthy of walking with Him and He will not remove their name from the Book of the Living and in the presence of his Father and all of his angels will declare openly that you belong to Him.

The message to Philadelphia pledges that He will keep them safe from the troubles coming to the world soon to test everyone on earth. He will make Philadelphia a pillar of the temple of the New Jerusalem which will come down from heaven.

John tells the church of Laodicea that they are poor, naked and blind. He advises them to buy gold from Him, pure gold in order to be rich and buy white clothing to cover up their shameful nakedness. John tells the church to also buy an eye ointment so that they could see Him in all his glory. He will rebuke and punish all that He loves that will give them the right to sit beside Him on His throne.

The prophet John then had another vision that took him to heaven. He found himself before a figure on a throne surrounded by the thrones of the twenty-four elders dressed in white and wearing gold crowns. From the throne came flashes of lightning and rumblings of thunder. In front of the throne were seven lit torches which were the seven spirits of God. In front of them was a sea of glass. John saw in the right hand of the One sat on the throne a scroll covered with writing on both sides secured by seven seals. Then he saw a lamb standing in the centre of the throne that looked to him as if it had been killed. It had seven horns and seven eyes which are the seven spirits of God that has been sent to the four corners of the world. Then the lamb was resurrected and took the scroll from the right hand of the One that sat on the throne and breaking open the first of the seven seals John saw a rider with a bow, wearing a crown sat on a white horse riding away to conquer the world. Then the lamb broke open the second seal and John saw a rider bearing a large sword on a red horse with the power to bring war to the earth. Then the third seal was broken by the lamb and a rider holding a pair of scales on a black horse appeared to John. A voice thundered,

A measure of wheat for a day's wages and three measures of barley for a day's wage, but do not damage the olive trees or vineyards.

Then the lamb opened the fourth seal and John saw a rider called Death on a pale horse with Hell following close behind. They had the authority over a quarter of the earth, to kill by means of war, famine and disease.

Then the fifth seal was opened and John saw underneath the throne all the souls that had been martyred for proclaiming God's word. Each had a white robe and were resting until the complete number of brothers had been killed.

Then the sixth seal was broken open and John saw a violent earthquake that turned the sun black and the moon became red like blood. The stars fell down to the earth like unripe figs, the sky disappeared like a scroll being rolled up and every mountain and island was moved from its place. John saw all the people of earth hiding deep in the earth in caves.

When the lamb opened the seventh seal there was a silence in heaven, then John saw the seven angels with seven trumpets standing before God. Another angel came forward filling his gold incense burner with fire from the gold altar and threw it down onto the earth causing rumblings of thunder, flashes of lightning and a great earthquake.

The seven angels with seven trumpets were now ready to blow them.

The first angel sounded followed by hail and fire mixed with blood to rain on the earth burning a third of all trees and vegetation.

Then the second angel sounded and a great mountain burning with fire crashed into the sea causing a third of it to turn to blood killing a third of all sea creatures and sinking a third of all ships.

Then a third angel sounded and a great burning star fell from heaven destroying a third of all rivers and lakes. The name of the star was Wormwood and it turned a third part of water to become poisonous and many people died of the bitter taste.

When the forth angel sounded a third of the sun's energy was lost and a third of the moon and a third of the stars were darkened. For a third of the day the sun did not shine and for a third of the night the moon and stars did not shine.

An angel then flew across the skies crying 'Woe, Woe, Woe' in a loud voice heralding in the three angels yet to sound.

Then the fifth angel sounded and using the star from heaven as a key opened the gates of the bottomless pit releasing the smoke of a great furnace that darkened the sky causing the sun to disappear. From out of the smoke came locusts that were like horses with faces of men wearing golden crowns on their heads and ready for battle. They had the hair of women and the teeth of a lion and wore iron breastplates across their chest. Their wings sounded like many horse chariots running into battle and their tails were like a scorpion with a sting to torment humanity. They were commanded not to harm nature but those people without the seal of God on their foreheads. For five months the godless will be tormented by the agony of the stings, seeking a death that will not come.

Commanding the locusts was the chief angel from the bottomless pit who the Hebrews call Abaddon, the Greeks call Apollyon and the Christians call the Devil.

After five months of torment, the sixth angel sounded and a voice from the four horns of the golden altar before God told the sixth angel to release the four angels that are bound in the great River Euphrates. The four angels were released to lead an army of horsemen totalling 200,000,000 to slay a third of all humanity. The army wore breastplates of fire and the heads of the horses were lions that billowed smoke, fire and brimstone and their tails were serpents. The two thirds of people who were not killed by these plagues and had not repented their worship of the devils and idols of gold and silver, brass, stone and wood, nor repent for their murder, sorcery, fornication and theft would suffer the fate of the seventh trumpeting angel.

Then another angel came down from heaven dressed in a cloud with a rainbow for a crown. His face was like the sun and his feet where pillars of fire with his right foot standing on the sea and his left foot on the earth. The angel roared like a lion seven thunders revealing seven secrets not to be written down and in his hand he had an opened book. John the prophet took the little book from the angel and ate it.

Then the seventh angel sounded and great voices in heaven were heard revealing that the kingdoms of earth shall become the kingdoms of the Lord and He shall reign forever and ever. The temple of God was then opened where the ark of His testament was seen before the voices became lightning and thunder, hail and another great earthquake fell upon the earth.

And then there appeared a great wonder in heaven, a woman clothed with the sun with the moon under her feet and a crown of twelve stars on her head. She was pregnant with her baby ready to be born when another wonder appeared in heaven, a great red dragon with seven crowned heads and ten horns whose number is 666.

I saw a woman sitting on the scarlet coloured beast spouting names of blasphemy, with seven heads and ten horns. She wore robes of purple and scarlet decked with gold, precious stones and pearls. She had a golden chalice in her hand that was full of the abominations and filthiness of her fornication. Upon her forehead were the words MYSTERY, BABYLON THE GREAT, THE MOTHER OF HARLOTS AND ABOMINATIONS OF THE EARTH

The angel reveals to John that the seven heads are the seven mountains on which the woman sits and the ten horns are the ten kings that have yet to receive their kingdoms. Each will hate the whore and make her desolate and naked; they shall eat her flesh and burn her with fire.

The dragon's tail cast a third of the stars in heaven to crash down to the earth and stood before the pregnant woman ready to devour her child as soon as it was born. The woman was given two wings of a great eagle so she could flee the serpent and hide in the wilderness with her son who was destined to rule all nations with a rod of iron. The wilderness was prepared by God to care for the mother and child for 1,260 days. Angry at losing his prey the red dragon cast out flood waters from his mouth to flush the woman and her son out from their hiding but the earth helped her by swallowing up the floodwaters before it reached the goddess.

Then another sign appeared in the heavens, seven angels filled with the wrath of God appeared carrying the last seven plagues to determine those of God and those of the Devil. They wore pure white and their breasts restrained with golden girdles. A great voice thundered commanding the seven angels to go out into the world and pour the rage filled vials down on the earth.

The first angel released her vial of wrath onto humanity causing ulcerous sores on the skin of those that had the sign of the beast on them. Then the second angel poured her vial into the sea destroying every living soul on the sea. The third angel made the rivers and lakes to become like blood and the fourth angel caused the sun to heat up and scorch the earth with fire. The fifth angel poured her vial onto the throne of the beast and his kingdom became full of darkness and the sixth angel poured her vial into the Euphrates whose waters dried up.

Then the seventh angel released her vial into the air and there were voices and thunder and lightning and a great earthquake struck the great city of Armageddon causing it to split into three parts. Then a great hail from out of the skies fell on the people of the earth until the darkness had been defeated and light ruled forever over the good and clean that feared the wrath of God.

Close Cousins

The Goddess of Love

Ask a hundred people what love is and you are likely to get a hundred different answers. For some it is a sickness and for others it is torment but for most it is a sweet bliss, a union with heaven. Love is in the air like a fragrant scent and people have killed for love and died for love. Love is many things; it is blind, it conquers all and makes the world go round. It will always find a way. Love will never be found by looking for it; it will find you when you least expect it generally after you have given up on it. Love hits you hard without warning when it does find you leaving the stomach feeling like it is full of nervous butterflies and a schoolboy/girl mentality takes over the mind.

A question I often ask myself is what does love mean to me? For one thing, it can mean the love for another person, a partner which, like the tide, ebbs and flows and like the seasons it can be hot and cold. Love changes as it grows and needs both partners to hold it together when love is stretched and insecure to be able to enjoy the bliss when it is strong. There is the love of your family because they are family and the love of friends who have your best interests at heart and love you for who you are despite your flaws. There is the love of animals and pets, a love of truth and knowledge, a love of adventure and nature. My girlfriend loves a clean house and she loves me and one of the best feelings in life is to be loved and true love is a two way thing, a love that grows as life changes. To be loved by those that you love is the most powerful energy in the universe.

Gods and goddesses never die; like a good wine they improve with age and reinvent themselves into better, more appealing powers that serve that moment in time. By the time of the Greeks rose to power in Eastern Europe as the empires of Asia began to disintegrate, the aging Ishtar recreated herself in Europe as

Aphrodite, which means 'born out of foam'. We are told in some stories that the Greek goddess of love was conceived in the foam of the ocean from the seed of Uranus that was spilt when he was castrated by Kronos for raping his mother Gaia, the Earth. Another story tells us that Aphrodite was the daughter of Zeus and Dione, the daughter of the Titan's Oceanus and Tethys who ruled over the planet Venus.

Around 1200BCE it was necessary for Ishtar to drop her virgin aspect and allow her lovers to live after sex, at least for a short while. The new goddess of love took great pleasure weaving plots to tempt the gods and goddesses into having love affairs with each other and to fall in love with mortals. She was constantly arousing passionate desires in anyone to amuse herself, sometimes getting in trouble with the other gods. Upsetting her father Zeus one day, Aphrodite was punished to fall blindly in love with a mortal man, a shepherd called Anchises. Believing that any mortal man that slept with her would prematurely age, Anchises was reluctant of any intimacy with Aphrodite until she reassured him that nothing would happen if they made love. She promised Anchises a demi god for a son, the Trojan hero Aeneas, who was the father of the royal line that was to build Rome after the fall of Troy.

A challenge was set in 1184BCE by a witch called Eris who gate crashed a royal wedding, offering an apple to the most beautiful goddess in the world. Was it Hera, the wife of Zeus, Athena, the sister of Zeus or Aphrodite, the daughter of Zeus? It was not a decision the king of gods was prepared to make so chose Paris, the son of Priam, the king of Troy, to pick the winner. Hera offered Paris kingship over Asia and Europe if he chose her, Athena would give him victory in all his battles and Aphrodite promised him the love of any woman he desired. After some thought Paris chose Aphrodite as the fairest of them all and wished for Helen, another daughter of Zeus and Leda, a Greek princess who was born from a swan's egg. The beautiful Helen just happened to be the wife of the king of Sparta, Menelaus at the time. Even before Aphrodite had finished eating her apple, Paris had whisked Helen back east sparking the great siege of Troy splitting the gods and goddesses and the heroes into taking sides and fighting against each other.

Meanwhile Aphrodite was looking forward to another husband. In return for his skills in jewellery making, Hera gave Aphrodite as a wife to the smithy god Hephaestus. As a present for his beautiful wife Hephaestus made Aphrodite a magic girdle that not only made whoever wore it irresistible but also acted as a shield that could withstand even the most powerful of Zeus's thunderbolts.

Marriage did not curb the mischievousness nature of the goddess of love. Angered because princess Myrrha refused to show respect to her father Cinyras, the king of Cypress, Aphrodite punished her with an insatiable lust for him. Disguising herself as a mistress, Myrrha spent twelve nights in the bed of her father until he discovered the truth and tried to kill her, forcing the princess to flee to the land of Sabaea where she appealed to the gods for protection. When they saw it was the doing of Aphrodite the gods turned Myrrha into a myrtle tree, the resin of which produces the fragrance myrrh. Ten months later the tree gave birth to Adonis who was delivered by a boars tusk. Adonis translates as 'Lord' in the Semitic tongue, the original title of Tammuz and misinterpreted as the gods name. Aphrodite saw that the baby was so beautiful that she had to save him so hid him in a casket and gave him to Persephone, the queen of the underworld to look after until he became an adult. Persephone, which means 'she who destroys light', was the goddess of death and another daughter of Zeus and half-sister of Aphrodite. Her mother was the fertility goddess Demeter. As Persephone, the transformed Ereshkigal experienced a happy childhood in the land of the living frolicking with other gods and goddesses. Persephone grew into a beautiful young maiden drawing the attention of the elder brother of Zeus, the god of death, Hades. The king of the underworld was given permission from his younger brother to marry his niece without informing Demeter. Claiming his bride Hades rode his chariot drawn by dark blue horses through an opening in the ground kidnapping the goddess when she was gathering lilies and carried her down into his dark kingdom. Learning of her missing daughter, Demeter was devastated and retired from the world to search the four corners of the earth to find her. The dark goddess Hekate points the grieving mother to the sun god Helios who reveals that Persephone was ruling the underworld alongside Hades. Enraged Demeter disguised as an old crone disappears in the wilderness to think of a way to get her daughter back. While she is gone, the earth became barren and nature began to wither and die. Zeus had to intervene before humanity would starve to death. Hades agrees to return his wife to her mother but before she left, the dark lord convinces Persephone to eat a pomegranate seed tying her to the underworld forever. It was left again to Zeus to sort it out ruling that Persephone would live on the earth from spring to autumn each year to live with her mother and spend the winter with her husband Hades in the underworld.

The Greeks celebrated festivals with Persephone and Demeter that corresponded to the life cycles of the grain and the agricultural seasons. At the spring ceremony, Persephone returns from the underworld causing new growth to appear above the warming ground heralding in the rebirth of nature. At the autumn celebration, Persephone descends into the underworld to protect the underground storage of the grain over the cold winter months.

Persephone looked after the baby Adonis in the underworld for her sister Aphrodite and when he grew into a handsome young adult, she fell in love with him. When the goddess of love came to claim him back, Persephone refused and declared

Adonis for herself causing the sisters to fall out creating a bad feeling both above and below ground. When sisters fight the whole world knows about it. In desperation, Aphrodite asked Zeus to sort it out, who ruled that Adonis would stay with Aphrodite in the land of the living for a third of the year, with Persephone in the land of the dead for a third of the year and live in the wilderness for the remaining third.

While with Aphrodite, Adonis ignored her warning not to attend the autumn hunt in the forest where he was fatally gored by a boar's tusk sending him to the land of the dead. This caused Aphrodite to leave the mortal world and go in search for him in the shadowy world of Hades, leaving the world without love. Zeus decreed that Adonis would return each year at spring when the red anemone was in flower to be with Aphrodite.

A major lover of Aphrodite was Ares, the god of war whom she had four children with; Eros whose arrow carries love to the heart of the person it strikes, Deimus the god of fear, Phobos the god of terror on the battlefield and Harmonia an ancestor of the Amazons.

With Hermes, Aphrodite gave birth to Hermaphrodites, the first female boy, a transsexual god and perfect balance of feminine and masculine energy and the gnome like Priapus who was famous for his enormous penis.

Aphrodite was attended by three beautiful young women called the Graces who served all of her needs. They were cheerful upbeat goddesses whose presence spread joy, sweetness and charm; Agalia, Euphrosyne and Thalia. They were nature spirits and are seen in the natural beauty found in a blooming nature.

With the rise of the mighty Roman Empire, it was a simple case of changing the names of the Greek gods and goddesses to suit their needs. Under the Romans, the goddess of love became Venus who was more dignified than her Greek counterpart. She was a queen of laughter and patron of social life and sensual pleasure. Other than that her life was pretty much the same as

Aphrodite's. Venus was the wife of Vulcan, the god of the forge who produced thunderbolts for her father Jupiter. Mythology reveals that Venus was born in the sea and had a scallop shell as a chariot that was drawn by swans or sometimes dolphins. She was the lover of Mars, the god of war who fathered her son Cupid.

Venus attained great prominence in the Middle Ages as the pagan earthly power that opposed the spiritual power of the church. Persephone became Proserpina whose grieving mother was Ceres the goddess of the harvest. Proserpina was kidnapped when she was a young woman by her uncle Pluto, the Roman god of the underworld.

At the same time, another empire was emerging in northern Europe, the Vikings. Ishtar emerged as the Norse goddess of love and beauty Freya, the daughter of Niord the god of the sea and winds and the frost giant Skadi. As Val-Freya she led the Valkyries down to the battlefield to claim one half of the bravest heroes killed to dwell forever in paradise alongside virgins and faithful wives. Freya, which means 'Lady' is normally depicted as blonde haired and blue eyed, wearing a corset over a long flowing skirt, a helmet and carrying a spear and shield much like the Greek goddess of war, Athena. Her husband was the sun god Odur but he grew weary of Freya's company over time and disappeared for adventure in the wide world causing deep heartache for the goddess of love. All of nature mourned for Freya as she went in search of her great love. After a long search and many adventures of her own Freya finds Odur in the sunny south in the shade of a myrtle forest and seeing him begins to smile again. As the reunited couple made their way home hand in hand the light of their happiness turned the grass green again, the flowers blossomed and the birds sang in joy.

When Freya was younger, she wished to possess the magic treasures made by four dwarfs but they refused to give her anything unless she made love to them. One treasure Freya obtained was a magic necklace that enhanced the wearer's charm; another treasure was some falcon feathers that allowed her to fly through the air like a bird that she used when she went in search of Odur. Freya was often seen soaring in the heavens in a chariot drawn by golden bristled boars with her brother Frey, which means 'Lord', sprinkling morning dew and summer light behind them. Freya shook spring flowers from her golden hair and scattered fruits and grain so that all the creatures on the earth could feed. Her tears fell into the rivers and oceans as rain so that all the creatures on earth could quench their thirst and cleanse their bodies and clothes. Freya used a chariot for her personal use drawn by cats, her favourite animal.

Freya needed rescuing once when she was promised by Odin as payment for the construction of a new wall at Asgard, the kingdom of the gods and was not aware that the builder was a giant in disguise until it was too late. The giant made his escape with the goddess of love on a magnificent powerful mare. The trickster god Loki transformed into a stallion to catch up with Freya and return her to a hero's welcome in Asgard. Subduing the mare and chasing off the giant, Loki mated with the horse that bore him an eight-legged stallion called Sleipner, which he gave to Odin as a gift.

Christians call the realm of the underworld Hell after its Norse queen of the dead Hel, another transformation of Ereshkigal. Like Persephone, Hel enjoyed a happy childhood with her father Loki, which means 'Flame' and her mother, the ice queen giantess Angur-Boda. She grew up alongside her brothers Fenris the wolf and Jormungandr the serpent in Jotanheim, living happily in the kingdom of the ice giants who continually sent out cold blasts of wind that would put nature into a deep sleep to rest for the winter. Loki kept his children and his marriage to the ice giant a secret from the leader of the gods, Odin because they were an enemy of Asgard. When Odin found out about the secret family, he had Hel thrown into the depths of Niflheim to rule over the nine dismal worlds of the dead. Iormungandr was cast into the sea and Fenris was bound with an Elvin chain and tethered to a rock on an island far off the coast of Norway.

The realm of Niflheim was situated to the north of a great abyss called Gimunga-gap, a vast deep chasm bathed in an eternal twilight. The bubbling spring of Hvergelmir at the centre of Niflheim supplied the twelve great rivers known as the Elivagar. The flowing waters would eventually reach the cold blasts of breath from the great abyss chilling the water into blocks of ice which rolled down into the great depths causing a continual rumble of thunder to echo and vibrate through the kingdoms.

To the south of the chasm of twilight was another realm called Muspellsheim, the world of the fire giants whose borders were guarded by the mighty fire giant Surtr. With his sword he sent showers of sparks to fall onto the ice blocks at the bottom of the abyss causing steam to rise where it would meet the prevailing cold and change into frost which, layer by layer filled up the great central space between Niflheim and Muspellsheim with ice from which the ice giants were born.

The freezing northern realm of mist and darkness was the kingdom of the spirits of the dead. For those warriors that died in glorious battle, their spirits enjoyed the comforts of Valhalla with the gods, but for everyone else who died naturally, accidently or diseased had to journey to the frozen north at death to dwell in a cheerless bliss with Hel. The criminal spirits would continue to the Hall of Nastrond to suffer extreme pain and suffering before being devoured by Hel's dragon Nidhug.

One of Odin's sons, Hermod the 'Swift', on his father's behalf once journeyed to the deepest parts of the underworld to plead for the release of his brother Balder, the young son god. After travelling for nine nights from Asgard, Hermod arrived at the golden arched crystal bridge that was suspended by a single hair and guarded by the skeletal maiden Modgud. The bridge spanned the great river Gióll that boarded Hel's kingdom and headed towards the deepest sanctums of the underworld to Gailler Bridge and Ironwood beyond, a land of iron leafed trees through which lies Hel's gate guarded by the fierce blood stained hound Garm. Inside the gate the seething waters of Hvergelmir nourished one of the three roots of a huge ash called Yggdrasil, the world tree of time and life. Its roots were fed by the waters of the three worlds; the bubbling spring of Hvergelmir in the underworld, the sacred well of Mimir in Midgard, the realm of humankind and the fountain of Urdar in the kingdom of the gods, Asgard. The falcon Vedfolnir perched on its highest branch keeping watch over the three worlds and reporting all that he saw to Odin. Scampering between the branches and the base of the tree a squirrel called Ratatosk passed its time spreading gossip between the falcon above and Hel's dragon below with the intention of stirring trouble between them. Gnawing constantly at the root taking nourishment from the river Hvergelmir the dragon Nidhug hoped to kill Yggdrasil knowing that its death would trigger the downfall of the gods.

Beyond the world tree, Hermod finally arrived at the many-roomed Halls of Hel where a bleak world with dishes of hunger, knives of greed and beds of sorrow awaited the guests to be looked after by a manservant called Idleness and a maid called ruin.

In her palace, Hermod stood face to face with the queen of the dead, a shadowy figure sitting on her throne. Hel stared back at the handsome god, watching him through her black shawl that hid her face that was half-distorted and rotted. Hermod told her that without the presence of the sun god in the land of the living all of nature mourned and ceased to grow. Hel agreed to release Balder on the one condition that if everything on the earth shed a tear for the sun god she will free him from death. An ice giant called Thok, who some believe to have been Loki in disguise, refused to grieve so Balder had to remain with Hel until Ragnarok at the end of the world.

When Ragnarok arrived Hel escaped her underworld prison with her faithful dragon Nidhug and the Hel-hound Garm to join her father Loki in the war against Asgard. After a long bloody battle between the two forces of light and dark, of good and evil and of life and death, Asgard was defeated. The wolf Fenris escaped his shackles belching toxic smoke over the earth and his brother Jormungandr the serpent flooded the world with one sweep of his giant tail bringing death and destruction to everything. Seeing that all was lost and the fragile balance of light and dark gone, the fire giant Surtr destroyed everything that there ever was in an inferno of fire of an almighty atomic blast.

The Queens of Heaven

It is believed that the biblical flood occurred around 5,000BCE sending the Anunnaki gods and their royal families, the priests and their chosen people to escape and settle high in the Caucasus Mountains between the Black and Caspian Seas that separate Russia and Asia. The people the Greeks called the Scythians, 'the Shining Ones' settled to the north of the mountains on the flat snowy steppes while the Cimmerians, 'the Noble ones' settled on the southern slopes until the flood levels receded when they migrated south into Turkey and then into the Mesopotamian deserts as the Sumerians around 3,500BCE.

The Scythians travelled westwards into northern Europe with their gods and goddesses to become over time Odin, Thor, Freya and the rest of the Norse deities we are familiar with today. They constructed great stone temples as they swept across the landscape towards the most western reaches of Europe to the Atlantic sea. At the same time another group of Scythians journeyed south eastwards tracing the foothills of the Himalayas to the Indus valley on the western fringes of the Indian continent to settle on the banks of the Indus River. They took with them the opposing forces of the sisters Aditi and Diti. Aditi which means 'Infinity' was the boundless heaven who embodied unlimited light and consciousness and depicted as the sacred cow of heaven. She governed the world with her dark sister Diti, or Finite, the dark serpent who constricted the life of humanity with her fixed earth bound laws.

Aditi was the mother of the Adityas, celestial deities that were the natural forces of the heavens that included the sky god Varuna and his brother Mitra the god of light. They regulated the movement of the sun, moon and stars and the winds and waters that cleansed and watered the earth. The children of Diti were the natural forces of the earth, elemental dark demons that caused earthquakes and volcanic eruptions that would destroy nature and everything in it. Between them they controlled the cycles of the seasons and the fortunes of humanity. Without darkness light cannot shine and without destruction rebirth cannot occur.

Sacred Indian texts reveal that the sky god Varuna created the world by picturing everything in his mind's eye. He possessed all knowledge and could control the destiny of the human race initiating the will of his mother the order that governed both nature and society. Varuna could see everything that went on in the world, read people's thoughts and sent messengers to oversee his wishes. The wind was his breath and the stars where his many eyes. After a thousand years of peace, a threat arrived in India around 1,700BCE when the Cimmerians migrated east from Mesopotamia and a great war broke out between the two powers as told in the Hindu sagas of the Rig Vedas. To strengthen his authority Varuna absorbed the separate powers of the Adityas into a single unit to become a powerhouse of energy, a super god called Indra.

We are told that Indra was born from heaven and earth, which separated forever at his birth. His mother was the earth goddess Prithivi who was depicted in the form of a cow and was the source of all vegetation. His father was the sky god Dyas, a red bull whose bellowing was the thunder who at night was seen as a black horse decked with pearls that represented the stars. A prophecy warned that when Indra was born he was destined to supplant the old order of gods so his mother Prithivi hid him away in a cave until he was old enough to look after himself. To help protect himself Indra received a thunder hammer from his mother.

Indra led the Devas, the gods and goddesses of light, divine beings into battle against the Asura invaders, dark beings who possessed supernatural powers. When the demons attempted to destroy the 'cow of plenty', partly by magic and partly by poison, the creatures of the earth went hungry because of the famine. Every living thing would have died if it was not for Indra and his twin brother Agni who removed the curse. Agni was the god of fire and born from a bolt of lightning who destroyed things so that new things can live.

Indra and his forces were conquered by the Cimmerians but managed to escape from India, making their way to the island of Crete off the coast of Greece to reinvent themselves as Zeus and the Olympians.

In Egypt the sky goddess Nut , the wife of the sun god Ra bore four children with her lover Geb the earth god; Osiris, Set, Isis and Nephthys. Isis was known as the goddess of Ten Thousand Names, one of which was the Queen of Heaven. She was the loving wife of Egypt's first pharaoh Osiris and caring mother to their son Horus. Isis was a faithful sister to Nephthys the goddess of 'death which is not eternal' and Set, an evil jealous god who longed to rule Egypt for himself. Isis was also a powerful enchantress who embodied the power of nature ensuring fertility and prosperity to the world.

Isis is the Greek translation of the Egyptian word Auset which means 'Throne'. Like Aphrodite, Isis had a mischievous streak, a dark side and liked to play tricks on the gods. Wishing to obtain some of the power of the aging Ra, Isis collected some of his dribble from his mouth that fell to the ground, mixed it with earth and moulded it into a snake. Causing the snake to bite the sun god and being so old Ra could not cure himself and was forced to reveal his secret name to Isis in return for a cure. With some of Ra's power, Isis became very skilled in the use of the magic arts. As a powerful sorceress Isis saved many deities and mortals from death using the power of Ra's secret name.

Her son Horus was conceived from the resurrection of Osiris after he had been murdered by Set who tricked his elder brother into a casket with no air and hid him in the delta marshes in the north of the country. Isis transformed herself into a swallow to search for her husband and after many months found him and restored his life by fanning him with her wings filling his mouth and nostrils with the breath of life. Then she transformed back into the goddess, sat astride Osiris, warming his body enough to awaken his sexual energy to conceive and returns him to a shrine in her temple. When Set discovered that Osiris was still in the land of the living he stole his body, dissecting it into fourteen pieces and scattering them across Egypt. With Nephthys and Thoth, Isis finds all the body parts except for his penis leaving Isis unable to conceive more children with Osiris. Thoth used his skills to stitch Osiris back together before Nephthys cleansed the body allowing Isis to bandage her husband to give Egypt its first mummified pharaoh.

Osiris had had enough of the harsh realities of the living world and went to rule the underworld. When Horus was old enough he revenged his father's death by killing uncle Set and taking the throne of Egypt for himself.

Isis was seen as the star Sirius that lines up with the belt of the constellation Orion. Sirius, aka the Dog Star, marked the start of spring and the coming of the flooding of the Nile. She represented the wind of heaven that personifies the power of spring instigating growth and yield again. In his guise of the grain, Osiris dies in the autumn and resurrected when he is sown over the land at spring.

Where Isis represents abundance, Nephthys signifies sterility and seen as the opposite to her sister in almost every respect. Where Isis was the essence of birth, growth and development, Nephthys was death, decay and apathy. Together they represent the things that already exist and the things that are yet to come into being, in other words birth, death and rebirth.

Nephthys was the mother of the funerary god Anubis, conceived when she tricked Osiris into sleeping with her.

The worship of Isis was spread by the Roman legions, traders and sailors throughout the Roman Empire alongside their own Queen of Heaven, Venus. Her popularity reached as far westwards as Britain and some believe she made it into India. Like Ishtar, Isis was seen as a big threat to the emerging patriarchal world after the death and resurrection of Jesus two thousand years ago and had to be destroyed.

With their origins in India a group led by their priest kings migrated west to arrive in Europe around 3,000 years ago. We know these people as Celts and their priest kings Druids. The Indian Aditi and Diti inspired the sisters Brigit and Cailleach for the European market. The root meaning of Brigit is 'Bright' and became to represent the fire of the hearth which kept the tribe warm and penetrated the dark, keeping the night at bay. Brigit was the fire of the forge that created metal weapons and tools. The Queen of Heaven gave the Celts the fire of inspiration and the ability to speak poetry and tell great stories around the hearth and campfires.

Brigit was the daughter of the Dagda, the father of all the gods who symbolised the new sun at daybreak. As well as representing fire, Brigit was also associated with water, residing in rivers, wells and springs. In modern paganism Brigit is generally seen as the three different aspects of the triple goddess; the maiden, mother and crone, or wise woman. As the maiden

Brigit experiences the world as a child would, with fresh eyes and an eager mind to learn everything. As the mother, Brigit turns her thoughts to nurturing and caring for her children, guiding them towards maturity and responsibility. As the crone, Brigit has the wisdom to teach the world from her experiences.

Brigit was associated with the Roman 'Queen of Heaven', Minerva. When they were not trading with the Romans, the Celts would have been at war with the mighty empire. Minerva, the goddess of wisdom and the patron of the arts was born out of Jupiter fully-grown and ready for battle. Her name is believed to mean 'thought' and stood proud dressed in armour guarding Rome with her lance. Minerva was based on the Greek virgin goddess of war Athena who was born out of the head of Zeus and according to Greek literature taught humanity the art of spinning and weaving at the end of the Neolithic period when hunter-gatherers became farmers. It was Athena we are told that tamed the savage nature of the Old Stone Age people by introducing arts and crafts to stimulate and enrich the human mind. She would go out of her way to help heroes on quests and reward bravery on the battlefield.

In her younger days Athena was linked to the Phoenician Mother Goddess Astarte, the 'Lady of Heaven' and wife of the rain god and lord of heaven, Baal. For the Hebrews Athena was Ashtoreth, a fertility goddess who was worshipped in Solomon's temple in Jerusalem 3,000 years ago as the 'Queen of Heaven' and wife of YHWH. With the arrival of Christianity, Ashtoreth suddenly became an evil demon, an abomination and charged with participating and encouraging sexual rituals and all things involved with joys of the flesh and a sin in the eyes of YHWH.

The Celtic Wheel of the Year

Brigit arrived into the world of the living at Imbolc at the beginning of February as a naive young maiden to instigate the start of spring, awakening the earth from her winter sleep. Imbolc sits midway between midwinter and the spring equinox in the northeast position of the wheel. Six weeks later at the spring equinox when night and day are balanced, the handsome divine son descends to the earth immediately catching the attention of the young Brigit causing the earth to blossom with nature to explode with new life. As the couple walked hand in hand across the land, their love grew like the plants around them. New born creatures frolicked in the leafy forests as the world bloomed in the strengthening sunshine and lengthening days.

At Beltain, midway between the spring equinox and midsummer in the southeast position on the wheel, the young couple marry and Brigit becomes pregnant with child. Her whole outlook on life changes, becoming protective of her precious unborn baby. Feeling neglected Maponos spends most of his time hunting wild boar in the forests. Whether fate or foul play at the midsummer celebrations Maponos is fatally injured during the summer hunt and returns to the otherworld leaving Brigit vulnerable and alone.

As the sun begins to lose power over the increasing darkness after the solstice, Brigit's belly begins to grow. Despite the dark eating into the light, the warmth is still powerful enough to bring the harvests to their conclusion. The first harvests at Lughnasadh instigate the start of autumn, positioned midway between midsummer and the autumn equinox opposite Imbolc in the southwest of the wheel. At the autumn equinox Brigit leaves the activity of the final harvest and descends to the underworld in preparation of the birth of her divine son.

As the nights draw in at Samhain, designating the start of winter giving the earth time to rest for a season. Samhain sits midway between the autumn equinox and midwinter opposite Beltain at the northwest position on the wheel. At the winter solstice, Brigit gives birth to the divine son who is immediately taken to be cared for in the Upperworld of the gods until he is old enough to return into the world of humankind.

After the birth, Brigit becomes the crone, the wise woman who will transform between midwinter and Imbolc into the maiden once more.

Cailleach remembers all that has gone before will be that which will come again. She knows she and the child will return into the physical world where they will fall in love again and marry. All she will remember when she arrives at Imbolc will be her name. She is Brigit.

Resting in Nature

To find any sort of balance in an ever-changing world, a journey needs to be taken; not only in the physical plane but also the spiritual realm. Our existence relies on opposing forces interacting with each other, a duality of a single energy, creating change that allows matter and life to evolve in space and time. It is a power struggle between two forces, a dynamic we witness with day and night, summer and winter and life and death. From the interaction of the duality, a third force is created from the first two, born as a separate energy, a new existence in the world of the four elements.

Ishtar and Ereshkigal were given life through the destruction of the Mother Goddess Tiamat, a boundless mass of ocean water that contains all the ingredients of life. Ishtar represents the infinite heaven. Her energy has the ability to heal and comfort those in need. Ereshkigal represents the finite and constricting underworld of the dead whose energy can bring death quickly to those suffering in life.

The sister's work together in order to maintain the balance of life and death, of light and dark and of pleasure and suffering felt in the human mind. Between them, they bring self-awareness and ambition into the material realm; their interaction with each other is what makes every mind unique to each person. They generate the change in the physical reality, creating space and time in which the human mind can interact in the realm of matter with what we believe to be free will. How they work together affects how things change in time, manifesting events through the attraction and repulsion of their force, invisible powers that play out in the physical world.

Today's world, for most of us at least, can be spent keeping a roof over our heads, having food and drink in our bellies and clothes to protect our skin from the elements. It is essential to be able to escape from the crazy world of taxes and laws, of politics and work, and journey to a sacred space in nature both physically and spiritually to wind down, release negative energy, relax, meditate and recharge the soul. There is a need to balance our material outer world reality with the spiritual inner world of the soul to bring harmony to both heart and mind.

I am blessed living where I do on Portland in Dorset on the south coast, a small island joined to the mainland by the famous Chesil Beach and a bridge and being surrounded by nature, cliffs, the sea, abandoned quarries and nature reserves. For a large part of the year the royal manor is inundated with tourists and it is difficult to find any peace and quiet anywhere at times. Luckily, Dorset has hundreds of ancient sites scattered across the landscape, many Bronze and Iron Age hill forts and Neolithic stone circles and dolmen well away from 21st century life to visit.

Our connection with harmony is found in nature, the physical proof of the god and goddess working together for the benefit of human existence. Close to where I live is the ruin of an old church built on Saxon foundations nestled in a valley on the edge of a cliff. On each side of Portland's first parish church sits two castles; to the north is Rufus or Bow and Arrow Castle, a medieval ruin of a fortress that once guarded the cove that served as an entry point between the cliffs for visitors and raiders to arrive from the sea. On the southern hill is Pennsylvania Castle, a gothic styled folly built in 1800 for the pleasure of John Penn, a good friend of George III wishing for a readymade ruined church and castle in his grounds. The old church was dedicated to St. Andrew in 1475 and has had a chequered history from its Norman beginnings with raids by French pirates, Vikings and disgruntled barons wishing to make a point against the monarch. St. Andrew's was abandoned in 1756 when nearby quarrying caused a massive landslip that twisted the church in two rendering it unsafe and losing half the cemetery to the beach below.

Today it is a hidden gem known only to locals and the visitors that like to explore the least travelled path along the coast. When I need to get back to nature, this is where I like to come. I spend the time between autumn and spring, when there are few tourists, cutting back the brambles, ivy and buddleia that cover the broken walls over the summer. I treat it as my garden, my sanctuary from modern life. I have witnessed handfasting and have been involved with witch circles here over the past eight years. Once my partner and I, Therese, decided to attend a Christian mid-summer sunrise BBQ at this sacred site where we ended up battling a raging storm coming up the channel. To me it was as if the goddesses that were once worshipped here when the Saxons settled on Portland were angry having been abandoned and ignored for the past 260 years by the Church. It was an interesting experience spent mostly trying to hold down the gazebo while listening to prayers asking for unity between all people and hellfire for the demonic pagans that they were aware used the sacred space. If only they knew it was a pagan that maintained the grounds and cleared the rubbish left behind by lazy visitors. I enjoyed a lovely bacon roll before they abandoned the church again to the wind and rain leaving me and Therese to call on the Celtic goddess Brigit, pregnant with the Divine Son at this time of year and a close cousin of the Middle Asian Goddess of Love, Ishtar. The earth was blessed with fire, water and air and because we were surrounded by the gravestones of early Portlanders, we honoured the ancestors that made the island and its people the community it is today.

When I can, sometimes with others but generally alone, I sit on the ruined wall that separates the chancel from the nave and meditate to the sound of the sea crashing against the cliffs and the waves sweeping up and down the cove below. I feel the wind against my face and listen to the trees rustling in the breeze and the bird song echoing across the valley. I breathe in the smell of nature and taste the sea air, interrupted occasionally by the engines of fishing boats chugging up the channel, exciting the seagulls into a frenzy, following in the hope of a feed.

Sometimes when I am working in the ruin I get a glimpse of someone in the peripherals of my awareness, watching my labours. I sense it is one of the ancestors buried here for over 300 years witnessing a pagan doing the work. My motivation is the goddess who was worshipped here by the Romans before the arrival of the Church. There is a belief that an alter to Venus once stood at this site, next to a pond that was fed by a river that flowed down from the top of Portland from a spring close to Kingbarrow. The river and pond has dried up now and much of the area has disappeared through erosion and extensive quarrying of the Portland Stone that went to build St. Paul's cathedral, 52 churches and most of inner London after the great fire of 1666.

During the tourist season I find it better to head to the mainland to escape the traffic and pollution and visit one of the many Celtic hill forts or Neolithic stone temples scattered across the countryside where civilization has not yet encroached with concrete and tarmac. I love these places for their isolation from the hectic modern world where we spend most of our lives.

One of my favourite Celtic forts to visit is Badbury Rings between Wimborne Minster and Blandford Forum in east Dorset. A Roman road once ran past from Bath in the north to Poole in the south with a fork north of the fort heading towards Dorchester. Badbury Rings is one of several sites identified as Mount Badon where King Arthur is said to have defeated the Saxons in 518AD. It is just far enough away from the main road to make the traffic noise a distant hum. The views from the ramparts are magnificent all round. Hidden villages surrounding Norman churches spread out in lush green fields separated by ancient Saxon hedgerows with a backdrop of rolling hills completes my transformation back into nature and releasing the pressures of the 21st Century from my consciousness. Sitting in peace and quiet, I can imagine the busy activity of the camp as it would have been like two and a half thousand years ago, seeing the Celtic people at work and play. I watch the guards walking the ramparts keeping watch over the landscape. Sometimes I might imagine a druid crossing the camp to his altar at the eastern edge of the fort.

My favourite Stone Age monument in Dorset is the Hellstone above Portesham below Hardy's monument. It is a Neolithic dolmen constructed about 4,000BCE and the oldest man made structure in Dorset. To reach it involves a muddy farm track, a couple of stiles and a field that is usually full of cattle but the views towards the south are spectacular revealing Portland in all her glory protruding out into the English Channel. In the winter, a large pond sits between the dolmen and a ploughed field. In the summer, the pond is a dried up crater between the Hellstone and a field full up wheat. Whatever the time of year it is an isolated site away from the modern world and the energy is strong, sometimes over powering to sensitive souls. On windy days I like to sit inside the ancient chamber to meditate and on warm sunny days I sit on the capstone to admire the view, slowly removing any negative feelings and replace them with the energy radiating from the Hellstone. I take myself back 6,000 years to when the dolmen was in use to wonder what its purpose was and imagine the effort it took for our Stone Age ancestors to construct it. It does not take long to find the peace needed to meditate to the tranquillity and sound of the countryside. I feel the air caressing my skin as I retreat inside myself to commune with the goddess and the earth spirits that dwell in and around the site.

Unfortunately, Dorset is not blessed with any great forests to explore and relax in but there is the Chapel Coppice at Ashley Chase above Abbotsbury where I love to spend time at to meditate. It involves a bit of a walk from Abbotsbury hill fort but is well worth the effort. Hidden in the woods are the remains of a chapel next to a small stream meandering from a tributary of the River Bride, a sacred river dedicated to the goddess Brigit and flows out into the channel at Bridport. There are enough trees and distance from civilisation to relax and engage with nature to balance the eternal forces of the goddess with the outer energies of the earth spirits who will reveal themselves to the meditating visitor. Be patient and be silent, be at one with nature and harmony will come.

After a visit to any ancient site I always come away feeling fresh and recharged by the energy of nature and the power of the goddess. All it takes is time and a desire for adventure.

The Unity of Duality

Our early ancestors saw the world organised into a trinity of unity, duality and a balancing force of the other two. The oneness of unity is the cause, duality is the opposing forces that create the change that allows humanity to exist in this elemental world of space and time and the balancing force is ourselves. The unity is universal love and the duality is Ishtar and Ereshkigal who influences our moods and emotions, our happiness and sorrows. Our moods and emotions change constantly throughout the day, throughout the week, the month, year and lifetime; it is human nature. It is the things that we cannot control that leads to frustration and anger causing us to lash out against the world, at our friends and loved ones.

The unity, the universal spirit, the will of the universe that some call god is the active initiating force +, the duality is the mind, the receptive processing energy – and the balancing force that is born from the first two forces is the physical human body.

During the Stone Age, the unity was the Mother Goddess who reigned over the mind compelling the brain to drive the body into action. With the arrival of civilisation, Mother Goddess became separated from the mind allowing the opposing forces to rule the mind unchecked for its own benefit. Without the calming presence of the Mother, the polarities are at constant battle with one another, struggling to overcome each other creating imbalance and conflict in the mind and dis-ease in the body.

When our inner energies are working harmoniously, the higher forces work with us.

The Babylonian priests understood the universe was made up of two complementary energies the ancient Chinese called Yang and Yin. Yang is the active principle with positive energies like Ishtar and Yin is the passive principle with negative powers like Ereshkigal. Yang is light and Yin is dark, Yang is above and Yin is below, Yang is fire, the outside, bright, dry, clear, expands, begins, initiates, is the bright southern slope of a mountain and the sunny northern bank of a river. Yin is water, the inside, dark, moist, hidden, contracts, concludes, receives, is the shady north slope of a mountain and the gloomy south bank of a river.

Everything is made up from these two principles; the differences between them are due to the different proportions of the dual forces. Every event in our lives is a result of the interaction between these two powers; the cause and effect of the universe.

The Chinese understood that all things in the universe from the stars and planets to the protons and neutrons are bound together by an intricate network of relationships that are continually interacting with one another. It stands to reason that anything you want to do, will stand a better chance of success if you work with these energies rather than against them. The two forces are never static and are constantly changing into something else, transforming both our inner spirit and our outer experience.

Each one of us has a purpose in life guided by invisible spirits driving our consciousness towards the events and obstacles we meet on our path. There are positive guides like Ishtar who radiates love, peace and happiness and negative spirits like Ereshkigal who spreads selfishness, greed and deceit.

Ereshkigal is our dark side. She allows the light of Ishtar

to shine in her shadow. When she is repressed, the dark side transforms human nature towards cruelty, corruption and conflict with others. The darkness can be seen as the physical realm of the five senses and the light as the essence of our being, our spiritual temple that connects with the rest of the universe.

To get the best from life, to rise above our daily challenges we need to find the balance of the two powers, find the fulcrum between the two, but the balance is not static and is constantly adjusting itself through the constant information it receives from the rest of the universe. To find balance it is important to hold both forces within your attention, seeing Ishtar and Ereshkigal together as a whole, to see both the positive and the negative aspects equally. Embracing the balance allows you to see the bigger picture helping to find the wholeness that leads to the truth and harmony.

Not everything is just black and white; most things are the many tones of grey in between. Like all opposites, love and hate, light and dark, hot and cold and right and wrong, there are many variations and proportions between the extremes that are changing all the time to be in tune with the universe. Taken individually they are life or death, light or dark and hot and cold. Together they are rebirth, shade and warmth.

As above, so below.

Balancing the Sisters

When I was studying photography at University, we had an exercise to explore the positive and negative aspects that can be found in images. We had to choose two photographs, one that portrayed a positive reaction within us and one that felt negative. Starting with the 'positive' image, we took a moment to examine the photograph before choosing an element of it that we found that made us feel optimistic and share it with the rest of the class. Then we examined the 'negative' image and chose an element that made us feel depressed. Then we returned to the 'positive' image and chose a negative aspect of it, then back to the 'negative' photo to find a 'positive' optimistic element in it.

I have replaced the photographs with Tarot or self-discovery picture cards for this exercise. I chose to use 'The Grail Tarot, A Templar Vision' by John Matthews and illustrated by Giovanni Casselli. For a bit of fun I am going to choose three cards that will represent my past, present and future for a general light look at things as they are at this moment.

The first card I pull from the pack is the 'Grail Seeker' or Fool. At first glance it appears neutral, a figure that represents the seeker of truth looks into the card towards the horizon. Between himself and a sea inlet is a large chasm that can only be crossed by the sharp edge of a sword spanning the abyss. In the heavens out of reach is the grail hovering in the sky. The seeker is eager and at the start of his quest. The vision of the grail is a positive, giving hope and reassurance that the quest can be fulfilled. Another positive is that once across the wide ravine it is an easy passage to the sea. Crossing the abyss on the sharp edge of the sword to begin the journey I see as a negative aspect.

The card means preparing for adventure with optimism and youthful carefree energy. It signifies a determination to discover the truth for oneself. Sounds about right for my recent past.

The second card is the One, or Ace of Swords. Spooky; swords are also spades meaning this card is the Ace of Spades which I am listening to now by Motorhead. A band of four black knights on horseback are fighting the seeker who is trapped in a cove surrounded on all sides by steep cliffs. In the distance is the walled city that the seeker has just left. The seekers sword glows with light and his face triumphant. At first glance this appears a negative card with the seeker about to be defeated by the armed knights. There is no escape. In all the negativity is the shining sword of the seeker; he knows the Shekinah, his goddess of light is with him. With her by his side the seeker knows he will prevail which gives him the courage to free himself from the situation.

This card represents triumph of strength over adversity allowing a push forward with incisive energy. I can't say my present is as dramatic as that but I have been there before.

Finally, the third card is the Ten of Vessels, or Cups, chalice or grail. A crowd of seven bare footed people including two knights and an angel gather around a priest in a high columned temple. The seeker is now the preacher and guardian of the grail, teaching the new knights and novices from his experiences. The seeker has reached his goal and is now the master. The imagery is one of success and very difficult to find anything negative in it at all.

The card represents the coming home after a long journey with a deep contentment and wholeness. The seeker stands at last before the Grail. I would settle for that thank you very much.

I could not have picked three better cards to reflect my past and hope for the future but as the goddess was my witness these are the cards I picked randomly from the pack.

By performing the exercise a few times with different cards will not only help you get to know your cards but also instil an awareness that within the positive could lurk a negative and within a negative generally hides a positive that can be found in all aspects of life. In any situation you find yourself in remember nothing is all good or all bad. A seed or spark of one energy is always in the other.

Bringing the Sisters into the Circle

After putting this book together, I feel confident enough in my understanding of Ishtar and Ereshkigal to perform a ritual in their honour; bringing them into a modern pagan circle. They are not, as far as I know, assigned to a direction but with their husband's they fit the four quarters rather well.

From the direction of the rising sun in the east, I place the Queen of Heaven Ishtar. I call on her to bring her light and love into the circle. From the east comes the element of Air, the precious breath of life and the essence of existence. Like the mind, the air is seldom still and can be anything from a gentle breeze to a destructive storm and everything in between.

From the south and the direction of the noon sun is the fertility god Tammuz. I call on him to bring fruitfulness and abundance into the circle. With the element of Fire, comes the spark of inspiration to bring new growth into the world. Fire is the drive and desire that pushes us forward.

From the direction of the dusk sun in the west is the Queen of the Underworld Ereshkigal. I call on Ereshkigal to bring with her the death that allows rebirth and evolution to occur. From the west comes the elemental waters that feed and nurture the seeds of Ishtar. Like the wind, Water can be a gentle flow or a destructive flood, which like the storm can bring transformation.

From the north of the dark sun is the god of war and destruction Nergal whom I call on to bring protection over the circle from any negative influences that may be lurking outside in the darkness. The north is the realm of the earth element that represents our outer reality, the experience of the physical world through our five senses. Earth is the realm of the beauty of nature and grounds the other three elements to the spirit of the planet. It is the earth element where both spiritual and physical reality connects.

Hail and Welcome

We have in the circle the forces of love, light, air, fertility, inspiration, drive, death and rebirth, nourishment, protection and grounding. Within that power is a little of myself and the others in the circle, now ready to make the transformation.

For the purpose of this chapter, I am inclined to dedicate the service to Ishtar on her feast day that rejoices the fertility of spring beginning to show in the land. We call this day Easter today, which is always held on the first Sunday after the first full moon after the spring equinox, anytime between March 22nd and April 16th. You can't get any more pagan than that. For the Christians it represents the death and resurrection of Christ and chocolate Ishtar eggs and bunnies, symbols of fertility. For the purpose of Ishtar and Ereshkigal, the most likely time to celebrate spring is at the full moon after the equinox.

At the centre of the circle is a blazing cauldron combining fire, heat and smoke with the restless energies called to the circle. Everyone in the circle has bought with them a personal wish written on a folded or rolled piece of paper and in turn drops it into the fire to manifest in the flames to release the energy into the air to be acknowledged and acted upon in the spirit world.

I call to lunar who has many names but I know her as the triple moon goddess Brigit at the stage of fullness as the radiant Red Queen bathing in the light of the sun. I ask her to help raise the energy in the circle skywards and into the heavens. Propelled by the wild dance between Ishtar and Ereshkigal and fuelled by the force in the circle. The power meets the welcoming hand from Brigit and kisses her, bouncing off her surface on its way to the source of the light on the other side of the earth. The power transforms into a physical reality in the sun to return in the sunlight to the earth the following morning. With the light and warmth of the spring sun, the wonder of nature awakens with fresh colour of yellow, pink and blue springing out from the lush green backdrop, radiating sweet fragrances to attract pollinators so they can be reborn. Arriving with the morning sun is the goddess of love to weave her magic into the fabric of the new day. She brings a love for all of humanity to share so we can see each other as brothers and sisters of the earth family.

Now rest in a moment of silence imaging a life of love, an existence of harmony where everyone is working together for the common good and respect for each other and the spirit of our planet. Imagine a selfless world without fear and injustice where everyone has a purpose, a home, food and drink within a loving and trusting society. Is it an impossible dream? Most probably but a dream is the first step towards the reality you wish to create for yourself. Willing it to happen is the second step and commitment is the third.

When you are ready, release any excess inner energy into the earth by touching the ground with your bare hand and be aware of your breath at the same time. Allow the rest of the senses to come back online before addressing the circle again. Thank the circle for their cooperation and participation and offer around a cup of mead or wine that symbolises the blood, the life force of all creatures for the circle to sip in turn and begin to relax and chatter quietly among themselves. It is a good moment to remember the importance of spring; without fertility there is no life, without love there is no fertility and without Ishtar there would be no love. The drinking of the life force is a blessing, an honouring of the supernatural forces that were attracted to the ceremony to become a part of that specific moment in time.

When the cup returns to its source it will be time to allow the spirits to leave and return the circle back to the earth.

Towards the east, I thank Ishtar for her presence in the circle. I thank her for her love and light before she disappears in search of others to spread her love.

Towards the south, I thank Tammuz for being here. I thank him for bringing fruitfulness and abundance with him before he to disappears, chasing after his wife with a bit of fertility of his own to see to after his recent freedom from the underworld.

Towards the west, I thank Ereshkigal for bringing rebirth and evolution to the circle. I thank her for not casting her evil eye over anybody in the circle before she disappears deep into the heart of the earth to her domain.

Finally, towards the north I thank Nergal for waiting patiently and alert protecting the circle. As he disappears into the night to take his place guarding the solar system from the demons that lurk in the darkness of the galaxy, the circle slowly reconnects to mother earth and return to the 'normality' of the 21st Century.

Hail and Farewell

If nothing else, hope was manifested by the ceremony, hope for ourselves, for everyone and for the planet. It is a positive manifestation of hope for the future.

Light and Dark

You make me laugh,
And you make me cry,
Between you both
I live, love and die.
I live for love
And will die for love,
I love to live
So my soul can fly.

I crawl like a snake,
And fly like a bird,
I ascend the tree
To discover the word.
As below, so above,
Like serpent and dove,
From dark to light
My spirit was lured.

Ishtar stands to my left,
Ereshkigal to my right,
One the goddess of love,
The other Queen of night.
Between them nearby,
In their shadows sits I,
Watching the cosmic dance
Between the darkness and light.

Epilogue

I thoroughly enjoyed researching and writing this book, it has led me to a better understanding of my connection to nature and the powerful forces within it. Without nature we simply would not be here. Without the elemental powers that strike lightning at the earth, erupt molten rock from within mother earth and supply the waters that flood the banks of rivers to provide fertile land for civilizations to live off we would not exist. All of these events would have needed meaning to the enquiring mind of the Stone Age people. By the Bronze Age these energies were translated as gods and goddesses with earthly forms and human personalities so the fertile human mind could picture the workings of the universe at a level they could understand it. They learnt to live alongside these powers as we would today famous celebrities. It was when pharaohs, kings, emperors and priests became the powerful gods themselves ruling the people alongside their less powerful goddesses, queens and wives that the balance changed in favour of the masculine force.

I have always loved nature and make my living in nature as a gardener and volunteer as a coastal ranger. For me it is about connecting with the earth, an earth that is full of wonderful treasures whose essence is a part of the realm of the gods and goddess energies. Writing this book, I discovered that Ishtar and Ereshkigal were key ingredients in the eternal cycle of the fertility of nature that gives life to everything living on the otherwise sterile planet earth. Their powers ensure that conception, birth, growth, reproduction, maturity and death can take place, ever evolving into a plan that has its source hidden and unknown to us mere mortals. The early fertility deities that included the sun who gave life to fire, wind and rain performed as a seasonal calendar to ensure harvests were abundant enough to last through the winter months of no growth. To ensure the return of fertility, a god had to travel to the kingdom of the dead to dine at the house of the Lord and Lady of the underworld until he is resurrected to bring love to the spring goddess and fertilise the earth between them. They were powerful forces then and are powerful energies now. They still transform something from out of nothing before destroying it and turning it into something else both physically and spiritually.

I am at that point on my path to recognise the invisible forces of the gods and goddesses are generated by the constant changing elemental forces occurring on earth merging with the cosmic powers from the solar system and the rest of the universe. An open mind can connect to these ever-changing energies constantly balancing themselves, allowing the consciousness to work with rather than against the universe.

As the gods and goddesses evolved over time so has humanity. We have no real understanding of the thoughts and beliefs of our ancient ancestors. I believe that the concept of love was different then to how we define love today and the same can be said about death. For us today, death is a sad event, it upsets those left behind because it feels as if a part of our own soul has departed with the deceased to an unknown destiny, a fate that every living consciousness has to experience. Our consciousness has been explained as an energy that is the mind of the personal spirit, and science tells us that no energy can be destroyed; only transformed into something else, something new. As I see it we are all connected to above and below, between heaven and earth from birth to death; our body and soul acts as a conduit allowing the two opposing energies to connect with each other. The interaction is experienced by our awareness in the realm we call life. Ishtar and Ereshkigal are the two forces that unite the human spirit to both the farthest reaches of heaven and the heart of the earth.

While writing this book I became very emotional, something generally not a part of my nature. I found myself shedding tears at films whether serious drama, comedy or cartoon where somebody 'overcomes' all the odds stacked against them to succeed through fate or sheer will to succeed, or win. I felt it was a reminder from Ishtar and Ereshkigal, encouraging me to be aware of my deepest feminine force whose passion is to respect the power, and sometimes the fragile state of nature, of humanity and of the planet. By opening up to the goddesses, I have opened the sensitive side of the feminine energy within my heart.

The only sure thing in life is that it will change. To experiencing the pleasures that life can offer it is necessary to learn of the suffering side to appreciate the good. We learn to be thankful for that we have good in our lives and always be aware that fate has a funny way of intervening sometimes. When things are bad and it feels as if Ereshkigal is smothering your determination remember, Ishtar is always nearby waiting to help pull you through the darkness. It is a common fact that light shines brightest in the dark; you will be noticed.

The universe is all about change, a transformation that spirals through creation, growing and destroying itself to constantly update and improve towards its perfection. To implement that change it is necessary for a piece of that original plan, what we think of as the soul that connects the consciousness of the human mind to the world of the god and goddess, the angels and fairies, as well as the demons and devils. This unifying spirit from the unknown source dwells within a suit of flesh and bones bought to life by blood so we can exist in this chaotic world of transformation ever needing order to grow and experienced through the five senses. Our brain is a physical organ that has become the controller of the spiritual mind that thinks the physical world is what reality is. Today the spiritual mind is seen as only a reflection of what our five senses tell us is important and thus real. It is what we perceive as real because that is how we are taught to believe.

Like the earth, we ourselves, individually and as a race are forever changing. Remember, once the earth did not exist, then it formed and has evolved over the past four and a half billion years to be as it is today. In the future, it will die and become dust for future worlds and future lives.

In the future, say three thousand years from now in 5019 what would archaeologist and historians make of our existence. It could be called the digital age, atomic age, the plastic age even? Would they see it as a destructive and polluted age or the age of God and man? Whatever they call our era they will discover the physical remains of our ritual places and ruined temples. They will also discover great regions of land cut out and mined for its ores and metals. Our descendants will also find a sense of order and cooperation among the population, a population that appeared to worship powerful gods and goddesses like e-bay the god of commerce and Amazon the goddess of shopping, communicating with them by 'the web'. Then there was Honda, the goddess of pleasure, and Citroen the god of travel and drive. Future humans might discover that the father of all the gods, the God of Knowledge, Google, who sat in the heavens on a cloud and could answer any question put to him via 'the net'.

Goddess knows what they will make of that.

Blessed Be
Imbolc 2019

Bibliography

Campbell, Joseph – The Power of Myth with Bill Moyers, 1988

Collins, Andrew – The Cygnus Mystery, 2006

Collins, Andrew – Gods of Eden, 1988

Cotterell, Arthur & Storm, Rachel – The Ultimate Encyclopaedia
  of Mythology, 1999

Eason, Cassandra – Ancient Wisdom, 2002

Freer, Ian – The Pagan Eden, 2013

Guerber, H. A. – Myths of the Norsemen, 1992

Hooke, S.H. – Middle Eastern Mythology, 1963

Hope, Murray – Practical Greek Magic, 1985

Icke, David – The Biggest Secret, 1999

Karcher, Stephen – The Kuan Yin Oracle, 2001

Lundquist, John M. – The Temple, 1993

Mackenzie, Donald A - Indian Myth and Legend, 2008

Parfitt, Will – The Complete Guide to the Kabbalah, 2001

Sitchin, Zecharia – The Lost Book of Enki, 2002

Souli, Sofia – Greek Mythology, 1995

Tate, Karen – Sacred Places of Goddess, 2006

Tresidder, Jack – Symbols and their Meanings, 2000

**MOON
BOOKS**

PAGANISM & SHAMANISM

What is Paganism? A religion, a spirituality, an alternative
belief system, nature worship? You can find support for all these
definitions (and many more) in dictionaries, encyclopaedias, and
text books of religion, but subscribe to any one and the truth will
evade you. Above all Paganism is a creative pursuit, an encounter
with reality, an exploration of meaning and an expression of the
soul. Druids, Heathens, Wiccans and others, all contribute their
insights and literary riches to the Pagan tradition. Moon Books
invites you to begin or to deepen your own encounter, right here,
right now.

If you have enjoyed this book, why not tell other readers by
posting a review on your preferred book site.

Recent bestsellers from Moon Books are:

Journey to the Dark Goddess
How to Return to Your Soul
Jane Meredith
Discover the powerful secrets of the Dark Goddess and
transform your depression, grief and pain into healing
and integration.
Paperback: 978-1-84694-677-6 ebook: 978-1-78099-223-5

Shamanic Reiki
Expanded Ways of Working with Universal Life Force Energy
Llyn Roberts, Robert Levy
Shamanism and Reiki are each powerful ways of healing; together,
their power multiplies. *Shamanic Reiki* introduces techniques to
help healers and Reiki practitioners tap ancient healing wisdom.
Paperback: 978-1-84694-037-8 ebook: 978-1-84694-650-9

Pagan Portals – The Awen Alone
Walking the Path of the Solitary Druid
Joanna van der Hoeven
An introductory guide for the solitary Druid, *The Awen Alone* will
accompany you as you explore, and seek out your own place
within the natural world.
Paperback: 978-1-78279-547-6 ebook: 978-1-78279-546-9

A Kitchen Witch's World of Magical Herbs & Plants
Rachel Patterson
A journey into the magical world of herbs and plants, filled with
magical uses, folklore, history and practical magic. By popular
writer, blogger and kitchen witch, Tansy Firedragon.
Paperback: 978-1-78279-621-3 ebook: 978-1-78279-620-6

Naming the Goddess
Trevor Greenfield
Naming the Goddess is written by over eighty adherents and
scholars of Goddess and Goddess Spirituality.
Paperback: 978-1-78279-476-9 ebook: 978-1-78279-475-2

Shapeshifting into Higher Consciousness
Heal and Transform Yourself and Our World with Ancient
Shamanic and Modern Methods
Llyn Roberts
Ancient and modern methods that you can use every day to
transform yourself and make a positive difference in the world.
Paperback: 978-1-84694-843-5 ebook: 978-1-84694-844-2

Readers of ebooks can buy or view any of these bestsellers by
clicking on the live link in the title. Most titles are published in
paperback and as an ebook. Paperbacks are available in traditional
bookshops. Both print and ebook formats are available online.

Find more titles and sign up to our readers' newsletter at
http://www.johnhuntpublishing.com/paganism
Follow us on Facebook at https://www.facebook.com/MoonBooks
and Twitter at https://twitter.com/MoonBooksJHP